THE STAR CHAMBER

HOW CELEBRITIES GO FREE AND
THEIR LAWYERS BECOME FAMOUS

THE STAR CHAMBER

HOW CELEBRITIES GO FREE AND
THEIR LAWYERS BECOME FAMOUS

ERIC DUBIN

The opinions expressed in this book are those of the author of this book and do not necessarily reflect the views of the publisher or its affiliates.

ISBN: 1-59777-553-3
Library of Congress Cataloging-In-Publication Data Available

Book Design by: Sonia Fiore

Printed in the United States of America

Phoenix New Millennium Inc.
9465 Wilshire Boulevard, Suite 315
Beverly Hills, CA 90212

10 9 8 7 6 5 4 3 2 1

TABLE OF CONTENTS

INTRODUCTION

Forty years in show business taught Michael Jackson one important lesson: never let anyone upstage you—whether it be 80,000 fans or 12 jurors. So when the day came for the young boy to take the stand against him at his criminal molestation trial, Jackson knew he needed a showstopper. And he delivered!

In one masterful stunt, Jackson and his lawyers managed, in essence, to silently rip the courtroom microphone away from the young accuser, with a headline-stealing visual:

"MICHAEL JACKSON WEARS HIS PAJAMAS TO COURT."

While it may not have looked planned, what you actually saw were his lawyers upstaging Johnnie Cochran's legendary, "If it don't fit, you must acquit" theatric. Think about it—what screams the message: "IT WAS JUST AN INNOCENT SLUMBER PARTY" better than baby blue pajamas and slippers?

Jackson and his pajamas became the headline of the day—and ultimately the trial—demoting the victim's detailed testimony to page 17 of most newspapers, along with the prosecution's only chance at conviction.

And there was so much more!

When it comes to high profile trials, Los Angeles has certainly developed a reputation around the world for getting it wrong. The California trials we watch on TV seem like Hollywood productions. The sensational celebrity story lines drown out the grim realities of the brutal crimes and innocent victims. The truth is, murder is murder, and yes, we out here in California take crime and punishment very seriously.

For example, the prosecutor who tried the Robert Blake criminal trial had never lost a murder trial before Blake. In fact, she had won 50 consecutive verdicts. The homicide detectives investigating Blake were 30-plus-year veterans, true California heroes who devoted their entire lives to keeping Los Angeles safe from horrific crimes.

So the question is: why do these celebrity defendants walk free despite overwhelming evidence of guilt that would undoubtedly convict you or me?

There is a very simple formula that is virtually unbeaten in celebrity trials: abuse the First Amendment outside court, and once inside, take the Fifth.

Over the years, every single aspect of these high profile media trials has been tainted by the media's involvement. The powerful spotlight affects every nook and cranny of the justice system. Everyone is affected by the glare of the cameras, from the plaintiffs and defendants, to the lawyers, judges, witnesses, jurors, and bailiffs.

The hourly hunger of the media for "breaking news" opens up an unbelievable First Amendment right to free speech forum, which lawyers use to contaminate the jury pool with misinformation that clearly would *never* be allowed in court. More and more, the lines between "news," "entertainment," and "justice" have become blurred. The media has now become a self-invited third player in the high profile trials of our generation, allowing famous defendants the opportunity to exploit our Constitution's First and Fifth Amendments. The end result is a constitutional tug of war between the media's right to free speech and everybody's right to a fair trial.

The power of the media also adds a new witness stand to the case—outside the courtroom. Without judges or rules of evidence, pretrial media coverage has become an open canvas for the smart and creative lawyer. A dangerous collaboration has formed between the justice system and the media, where conflicting objectives inevitably taint the sacred process.

High profile trials have proven to be media gold mines, real unscripted dramas with unbelievably huge stakes. Live on TV, 12 everyday people decide whether an American icon lives the remainder of their life in a mansion or a state prison. Celebrity trials have almost become another one of Hollywood's million-dollar exports, generating huge fascination among American citizens, as well as attracting a worldwide following.

New seasons followed the O.J. saga, with the high profile cases of Robert Blake, Scott Peterson, Michael Jackson, Phil Spector, and others. During the Jackson verdict, ratings absolutely soared on all the cable news networks, with MSNBC's ratings going up 80%, and both FOX and CNN doubling their audience. In fact, following the verdicts in the Jackson trial, the Associated Press reported that the three cable news networks pulled in 10 million viewers at a time slot during which they would normally have had less than two million people watching.

These mega trials are stories people like to watch on TV, read in magazines and papers, and take to the water cooler. Scott Peterson took the genre to a new low, with the media demonstrating high profile trials can still sell magazines and increase ratings without a "big name" star. Since Peterson fit the image of young, good-looking Hollywood, he was cast to fill the celebrity void during that time. In short, the mass media trumped up a handsome, murdering cheater named Scott Peterson from Northern California and made a gold mine out of nothing.

While high profile trials from Lizzie Borden to Charles Manson were certainly always a huge source of public fascination, modern technology had not yet evolved to allow the public intimate access to all the details inside the court. We have become a reality TV society, and nothing is more real than a beloved celebrity facing life in prison.

One thing Johnnie Cochran fully understood was that every jury panel is made up of 12 people who have grown up in the TV "sound bite" generation. Specifically, it's all about storytelling and visuals. Cochran also understood winning *outside* the court with the public was directly related to winning the case *inside* with the jury.

While in the L.A. County Jail awaiting his murder trial, Robert Blake was recorded giving an incredible narrative of his feelings towards the potential jurors in his trial. In talking about his then-lawyer, Harland Braun, Blake was taped through a concealed recording device within the jail walls saying:

"He's [Braun] a good lawyer. He's a great lawyer. I worry about him and a jury because he doesn't have that one quality that genius trial lawyers have, that understand that people who sit on a jury watch wrestling and they bowl and they eat pizza and they drink beer.

"Johnnie Cochran was a genius of that. Like certain people like Jesse Jackson is great at understanding those people. Because anybody who has a job that they care about does not get on a jury. Anybody that has a life they care about, anybody that has a wife they care about, they just don't get on juries. They get called, and somebody will say, 'Well, do you believe in the death penalty?' [And they will] say, 'No, I believe that Jesus should kill everybody.' 'Okay, goodbye.' So they all leave.

"And the ones who stay are usually about 85 IQ and, you know, when Johnnie Cochran stands up there and says, 'If it doesn't fit, you must acquit,' we all thought he was a fucking idiot. But the jury digs that because they're the people that go bowling."

USA Today recently ran a list of the 25 most memorable quotes of the past quarter century, and number one on the list was "Let's Roll" from American hero Todd Beamer on doomed United Flight 93. The second quote was Ronald Reagan's appeal to the Soviet Union: "Mr. Gorbachev, tear down this wall!" Coming in third on the *USA Today* list was the late Johnnie Cochran and his classic line: "If it don't fit, you must acquit."

When the O.J. Simpson trial took place, the outlets were fairly limited. You basically had CNN and the major networks. Not only has the whole Internet explosion occurred since O.J., but you also have literally a half dozen or so shows specifically devoted to high profile trials. Much like recent exposures of questionable behavior by many in Washington D.C., today's media omnipresence has made it virtually impossible for major indiscretions or crimes to happen on such an invisible level.

In other words, the old dynamic of powerful Hollywood studios protecting their number one commodity (celebrities) through cover-ups, before charges could even be filed, are virtually gone. What still remains is the power of fame over a "jury of our peers," and the vast difference in the results of these cases.

The "power of fame" with respect to special treatment in jury trials only works if you are a celebrity. The most recent example of having false illusions of celebrity justice was Scott

Peterson and his lawyer, Mark Geragos. Scott Peterson was *not* a celebrity; the glare of the cameras and attention clearly blinded his defense team into believing they had any fame chips to cash in with the jury. They did not!

I spent over five years working on the Robert Blake case, and won the 30-million-dollar jury verdict against Blake for killing his wife Bonny Lee Bakley. The first three years I spent on the case were primarily consumed by having to deal with the media. It was up to me to level the playing field after Blake's massive victim-bashing campaign.

Over the years, I personally battled almost a dozen of Blake's high-power lawyers, both inside and outside court, including the legendary jailhouse fight with Tom Mesereau before he left the case to win the Michael Jackson trial.

I was in court everyday and held the victim's daughter, Holly, when the Blake criminal jury read the "Not Guilty" verdicts for the murder of her mom. Eight months later, alone, I proved to our jury that Blake *did* in fact kill his wife. Against all odds, I beat the huge law firm defending Blake (led by the managing partner Peter Ezzell, who had a jury record of 150-3 since 1970).

I was followed by cameras and reporters everyday during that trial, scrutinized from the minute I opened my car door until I left at the end of the day. With Blake and his lawyers to my left, the jury to my right, and the worldwide media sitting five feet behind me, no flaw would go unnoticed—and that's not even mentioning the judge sitting directly in front of me.

I have also spent years serving as a legal commentator for CNN, Fox News and Court TV, providing analysis on some of the biggest headline trials of our time. I have been quoted in newspapers around the world, and have come to understand all angles of the latest mega trials.

Our trial judge in the Robert Blake wrongful death case, Judge David Schacter, always used to say, "There are two separate cases going on here: one inside the courtroom and one outside the courtroom in the media." He was absolutely right. And you need to win both!

Accordingly, the corridor that leads the way to the Star Chamber is not located within the courthouse. The winding path that leads to "celebrity justice" begins with the media.

CHAPTER 1

WHY DO STARS GO FREE?
THE WINNING FORMULA

In the history of Hollywood, no major celebrity has ever been convicted of a crime and sent to prison. Nobody! Yes, there have been a handful of Robert Downey Jr.'s, who have resided in L.A. County Jail on drug charges for a short time, but they have never spent hard time in a California state prison.

The major stars who have been involved in the recent mega trials were all-American icons that had accumulated many years of good will celebrity chips. Blake had about fifty years of entertaining under his belt (along with the gun he "left at the restaurant"). O.J. was a local football hero at USC before NFL greatness and hurdling through airports for Hertz. Obviously the same is true of Jackson, arguably the most famous person in the world at the time of his trial.

It makes you wonder if, after so many years of entertaining the public, they felt entitled to a free "get out of jail" card.

As it turns out, apparently they were. All three stars basically walked over to the cashier at the end of their criminal trials and cashed in their lifetime of accumulated fame to walk free. Blake flaunted his "she had it coming" defense for years before trial, implying that he deserved a break because he was famous and Bonny was a "bad person."

So, why did all these famous defendants skate free despite devastating evidence of guilt against each of them? The first answer may be obvious, but it is the core of the problem: they got special treatment from the jury.

The justice system is simply not designed to work for a celebrity defendant, and, in fact, American courts are built upon a contradictory foundation. The entire premise of jury trials is for 12 strangers who have no knowledge of—or history with—the defendant, to objectively listen to both sides and render a verdict.

One of the first steps in the jury selection process of all trials is to immediately get rid of potential jurors who know any of the lawyers, witnesses, or participants. The idea is they could never be truly fair and objective if they already had an affiliation with—or extraneous information about—anyone involved in the case.

There rests the first major problem.

The jurors in these celebrity trials bring in decades of familiarity with the career and life of the celebrity defendant they are being asked to judge. Before the process has even started, jury selection has been fatally flawed.

America is rich in pop culture and loves its celebrities—actors, athletes, or musicians alike. We grow up watching and following our favorites, and reward the best with fame and fortune. Many of us even equate songs and movies with special moments in our own lives. I have drawn the analogy that asking a jury to put a major celebrity away in prison is just like asking them to convict a beloved friend. Much like if it was a friend whose freedom was at stake, jurors give every benefit of the doubt to the defendant. What happens is the legal standard of "beyond a reasonable doubt" gets elevated to an impenetrable level. Think about it, would you send a dear friend to prison for a crime if you were not 100% sure? Without a point blank video, can anyone ever be "absolutely sure"?

I can tell you how horribly frustrating it is for a victim's family to hear these jurors say—post-verdict—that they personally feel the celebrity defendant committed the crime, but could not convict "beyond a reasonable doubt."

Another relevant factor in celebrity trials is the extreme difference in appearance between celebrities and the average person. I am not sure if these people become celebrities because they truly have something special about them, or vice versa, but more often than not, they possess a charisma you don't normally see in accused murderers. You simply don't have the urge to ask your garden-variety criminal for an autograph, yet alone to pose for a keepsake picture.

The power of being a celebrity also affects how the entire courthouse staff treats a defendant, and this does not go unnoticed to the ever-watchful jury. If an information-hungry juror watches a bailiff smile at Jackson, or say good morning to Blake, there is so much that can be read into it.

Jurors sit in court six hours a day. There is plenty of time to notice everything, and most do. For example, in an average criminal trial, they might watch if a wife or mother comes to the trial to support the defendant, and if there is love evident in their interactions with the accused.

Let's face it, the usual murderer is brought into court in shackles, and treated like a criminal by all but their lawyer and family. A celebrity defendant walks into a courtroom, and they are treated like a celebrity.

In these high profile trials, you also have a media all-star team sitting in court, openly talking and joking with the famous defendants. Obviously each journalist is just trying to get an interview with the accused, but the fact of the matter is that the jury observes all the signs of admiration.

A fatal misstep for the prosecution has been trying to treat these cases like any other, despite the obvious reality that jurors don't treat celebrities like everybody else. In fairness to the prosecutors, there appears to be a double standard in play with respect to what a state prosecutor can get away with in pretrial media statements when compared to a defense lawyer. A recent example is the disbarment of the D.A. in the Duke lacrosse rape case for pretrial comments made to the media about the suspects.

Clearly, the high profile defense lawyers were the first to figure out how to tweak the celebrity justice system. O.J. created a blueprint for winning these celebrity trials, which over the years has needed very little modification.

Basically, there are four steps to sure-fire celebrity freedom; a formula that is virtually unbeatable in California's high profile trials:

1. TAKE THE FIFTH AMENDMENT AFTER ABUSING THE FIRST
2. BASH THE VICTIM AND ALL THE "MEDIA-TAINTED" WITNESSES
3. BLAME THE "FAME-HUNGRY" POLICE
4. HIRE TOP EXPERTS FOR "THE CSI EFFECT"

TAKE THE FIFTH AMENDMENT AFTER ABUSING THE FIRST

Full media access is an unbelievable fringe benefit of being a celebrity, and allows criminal defense lawyers to plant critical seeds of doubt into the minds of the public. The basic idea is to have your defense lawyer utilize their jury-tainting opportunities under the First Amendment before the trial even begins.

Once your message has been heard loud and clear and the time comes to go to trial, the next winning move is to stay mute under the Fifth Amendment right to remain silent. Thus, the road to celebrity freedom starts with the basic equation:

The First Amendment power of celebrity +

The Fifth Amendment right to remain silent = <u>freedom</u>.

The main reason you never see a famous defendant take the witness stand at the criminal trial is that the Fifth Amendment right to remain silent forces a jury to convict a beloved celebrity without hearing an answer to the most important question: "Did you do it?" Again, could you convict a close friend without him or her getting a chance to explain or deny what happened?

A "normal" accused murderer who takes the Fifth Amendment would be considered unable to withstand the prosecutors' cross-examination and condemned by the jury. Celebrities simply look like they are following the advice of their high-powered lawyer. Unlike a normal criminal defendant, when a celebrity takes the Fifth Amendment it actually strengthens the argument of "reasonable doubt" for the jury. The reason is that the jury has no direct harmful evidence from the defendant's mouth to offset their preconceived notions. Taking the Fifth Amendment allows a celebrity's idealized body of work to be the only insight a jury has. Talking about the alleged crimes can only take that away from the juror's pleasant walk down memory lane.

When done right, a lawyer can resourcefully present his client's testimony to the jury pool through the media using the First Amendment, and then avoid any damaging cross-examination under the Fifth. An expert lawyer can present the defendant's testimony to the jury pool without ever even entering a courtroom.

A major mistake made by Peterson's defense was attempting to follow this celebrity formula of silence—Peterson was never a celebrity. There is no question the jury needed to hear him speak out on the stand because when they looked at him they did not see a beloved celebrity; they saw a smug asshole that killed his pregnant wife.

Peterson's lawyer, Mark Geragos, made a huge error by confusing the glare of extreme media coverage with the entitlement to follow the celebrity blueprint. Geragos should have realized Peterson had no fame chips to cash in, and without them, obvious guilt usually leads to unanimous convictions. That is why Peterson lives on death row. That, and the fact that *he killed his beautiful wife and baby.*

BASH THE VICTIM AND ALL THE
"MEDIA-TAINTED" WITNESSES

The second prong to celebrity freedom is using the defendant's fame chips to win credibility contests against all of the witnesses, and even the deceased victim. O.J.'s lawyers tested the waters of victim bashing with his dead wife, Nicole Brown Simpson, leaking to the media that she hung out with "coke addicts and drug dealers." One of them went so far as to publicly blame Faye Resnick's alleged coke dealer for the murder.

O.J.'s "dream team" proved that the public would even tolerate celebrity lawyers taking an offensive posture against the victims themselves. Following O.J.'s case, defense lawyers in celebrity trials realized that jurors had a stronger feeling of compassion for the celebrity defendant than the victim, so they could get away with a little dirt.

Over the years, victim bashing has become absolute celebrity trial 101. Most of the appalling conduct occurs outside the court, either through formal press conferences or by secretly leaking information to the media. It is terribly unfair to both the silenced victims unable to defend themselves, and their families forced to watch.

Under the First Amendment, evidence and information that defense lawyers surely know would be inadmissible at trial can be freely aired to the jury pool through the media with one simple criteria: it will generate ratings.

In both the Blake and Jackson cases, victim bashing was pivotal to winning. Blake's lawyers worked the "she had it coming" defense for almost three years before trial, totally unopposed in their media campaign for a full year before I was hired on behalf of Bonny's four kids.

I cannot remember a single interview I have done over the years about the Blake case where I was not asked in one way or another: Isn't it true Bonny was a horrible person who had this coming? Granted, nobody ever quite phrased it that way, but that was basically the undertone.

The second huge ramification from the media's involvement in these high profile cases is the media *itself* contacting and tainting the potential witnesses. Obviously, in any trial, the job of the lawyer is to impeach or discredit witnesses against their case by any legal means possible. Primarily, the biggest punches a trial lawyer has are claiming the witness is biased or has alternative motives for testifying.

Accordingly, the media itself plays a huge role in tainting the witnesses in every high profile case just by interviewing them, with or without pay. The cross-examination goes something like this:

"Let me show you what we will mark as exhibit 'A.' It's your absolute lack of credibility by way of a copy of the interview you gave to *Star* magazine. How much were you paid to sell your 'story'?"

Everybody wants their 15 minutes of fame. OK—at least most people. Trust me that I fully understand how extremely hard it is to say no when the *Today Show* calls you on your cell phone to come on their show. I never did.

So, what the high profile defense lawyers have learned to do is capitalize on the media circus on both ends, making double use of the First Amendment. They jump to use the media to plant the critical seeds of their defense, and then scream "taint" when anybody else follows suit.

Once a witness speaks to any media before trial, the dynamic completely changes, and the celebrity defendant is viewed as a victim of "fame-seeking" witnesses. Even if that witness is completely telling the truth, or only speaks to "reputable" news programs, media contact always creates devastating impeachment:

"Now isn't it true you went on *GMA* with this story you are now telling this jury secondarily? And then you went on CNN, then you went on Fox News…. True? How many times did you go on TV to tell your sensational story before coming into this courtroom today? Did *GMA* send a limo for you? Did it have bottled water? In fact, isn't it true you told your story to local news the night of the incident, before you ever even talked to the police?"

Is it really fair to blame people for wanting their 15 minutes of fame, or to even expect them to turn it down when it literally knocks on their front door? How can you expect an average person to reject an easy $10,000- to $20,000-dollar payday just for telling the truth about what they know?

I really believe that an average person would not lie and risk sending an innocent person to prison for the rest of their life just to get their name in a tabloid. But the defense works that angle, and works it well! In these high profile trials, once again, the First Amendment inadvertently plays a role in hampering the pursuit of justice.

BLAME THE "FAME-HUNGRY" POLICE

Ever since the O.J. trial there has been a built-in defense for all high profile cases in Los Angeles, and it is *not* race. The post-O.J.-trial defense that has been a high profile case fixture for the past fifteen years is: "This was a rush to judgment because the LAPD and D.A.'s office was desperate for a big conviction to make up for the O.J. verdict!"

The ghost of O.J. still creates problems for the police, who are no longer "racists" but "fame seekers," who will do anything to take down a big celebrity because of the O.J. stigma.

In most trials, when a police officer takes the stand, his testimony carries guaranteed credibility. However, in high profile cases, this standard is reversed, and members of the police force are far more susceptible to fierce cross-examinations. Defense attorneys routinely spin an argument of the police being hungry for the glory of major convictions.

Robert Blake definitely understood how important it was to bash the police before and during his trial. On one occasion, while in jail, he was recorded discussing what he thought his lawyer, Harland Braun, should be doing for his defense.

"Let Harland get dirty. Harland's job is to show how bad the cops are and how bad Bonny is.... Your job is about me and Gavin [*Love Boat* Captain] and the old days, and I'm not the person they painted me out to be."

In the Phil Spector murder trial, Spector's famed New York mafia lawyer, Bruce Cutler, repeatedly played this angle in his opening argument. Cutler aggressively argued to the jury that the LAPD had "MURDER ON THEIR MIND, MURDER ON THEIR MIND."

I actually believe Spector's lawyer was absolutely right with respect to the facts of his case. When a man walks out of his house with a bloody gun in hand, and a dead woman in his foyer, saying he thinks he just killed somebody, the police *should* have "MURDER ON THEIR MIND, MURDER ON THEIR MIND."

HIRE TOP EXPERTS FOR "THE CSI EFFECT"

Question: What are three things Robert Blake and Phil Spector had in common?

i. Neither of them had an alibi when the women they were with mysteriously got shot in the head;

ii. They both had gunshot residue on their hands immediately after the shooting;

iii. In both cases, the State conceded it could not prove who fired the murder weapon.

When it comes to winning a trial, whatever power "fame" lacks inside a courtroom, "fortune" makes up for twofold. Fame awards a defendant the benefit of the doubt when it comes to condemning evidence against him, while fortune buys him any corroborating expert opinion they could possibly need for their case.

The ability to spend liberally on a scientific expert is an undeniable advantage in every trial. You often hear prosecutors complain about what they call "the CSI effect." Basically, the concern is that when jurors watch today's crime shows, they develop unrealistic expectations of the scientific evidence that can be presented. Jurors anticipate some form of scientific smoking gun, and unfortunately, real trials are not hour-long shows with clean endings.

The "fortune" part of fame and fortune can pay for the best experts in the world, making the prosecution's burden of proof all the more challenging. For the right amount of money, specialists can contrive "reasonable doubt" by finding grey areas in almost all scientific areas, or by pointing out how little evidence the prosecution has. Likewise, creative forensic test results can be bought to corroborate the "scientific" trial testimony needed to win a case. Technology has evolved to allow us to TIVO every show on the planet, and load a lifetime of songs into a Tic Tac box, but we cannot yet ascertain who fired a specific gun.

Robert Blake had the infamous alibi that he was busy getting his gun from the restaurant when his wife was shot in his car. Blake did in fact have a gun on him at the time of the killing, and then turned it over to the police that night, after the shooting.

Because of scientific limitations, the police had to exclude the positive gunshot residue (GSR) results found on Blake's hands and clothes after the killing. The reason being that they could not determine which gun the residue was from—the murder weapon or Blake's "other" gun.

My understanding is there is no scientific way of differentiating gunshot residue between one gun and another. To make things more complicated, a gun gives off a different amount of gunshot residue every single time you shoot it, with no rhyme or reason to the quantities. Accordingly, there is no number of particles a defendant should have on him if he fired a weapon; it could be twenty, or it could be twenty thousand, it changes with every shot.

GSR is also like sand. It can be washed off the hands and skin easily, although it often clings to clothes for a very long time. A clever lawyer can blame GSR on clothes from events unrelated to a shooting, such as simply carrying a gun, hunting, or even police contamination. In Blake's case, because the police put all of Blake's clothes in one bag, the defense successfully argued cross contamination.

In Spector's case, the defense experts argued that the victim had more gunshot residue on her hands than Spector did so it must have been suicide. There is no question the residue on the victim's hands could have come from obviously trying to shield her face before being shot. There is also no question that Spector could have easily washed his hands, when his victim quite obviously could not. It can be argued both ways, and that alone can be enough to create reasonable doubt.

There was no dispute Blake had gunshot residue on him immediately following the killing. I explained the gunshot residue issue to my jury in very simple terms: "I don't have any gunshot residue on me right now; do you?"

MURDER (TRIAL) BY NUMBERS

Let's apply my celebrity acquittal formula to the specifics of three of the most recent high profile celebrity trials of our times: Michael Jackson, Robert Blake, and Phil Spector.

First, imagine if any of the basic contentions presented in those cases fell upon *you* when called for jury duty, but the charged defendant in your case was not a celebrity. You see the defendant sitting with the public defender: a 44-year-old, androgynous-looking male wearing lipstick and heavy make up with armbands around his jacket sleeves.

Without even knowing the charges, you are already thinking: *"Wow, this guy looks guilty of something!"*

You remind yourself not to judge a book by its cover and wait to hear all the evidence before making up your mind. You then learn from the court the following information about the case you are to judge:

The Defendant is MJ, an unmarried 45-year-old local singer and dancer. He has been charged with seven counts of child molestation upon a 13-year-old boy, a felony, in addition to serving alcohol to the said minor. The alleged molestation took place in the defendant's bedroom in his secluded ranch.

The defendant, MJ, admits to having the accused, as well as numerous other 13-year-old boys, sleep over at his house and share his bed. The defendant claims it was just harmless fun—the boys are lying. You will hear testimony from several young boys, who will testify that the defendant MJ had molested them in the past, one boy having previously accepted a large settlement. The defendant will be taking the Fifth Amendment and will not testify on his own behalf.

OK, let's start with the obvious: A 45-year-old man with a 13-year-old-boy fetish, sharing his bed with young boys—unsupervised.

Can you say: "Bailiff, we have *already* reached a verdict"?

In the real case, MJ was not a typical creepy accused pedophile defendant—he was Michael Jackson, the *famous* creepy, accused pedophile defendant.

The first prong to Jackson's path to freedom was using the First Amendment freedom of speech to plant the seeds of his defense. Michael Jackson's legal strategy to use his unprecedented access to the worldwide media is so legendary that it deserves its very own separate chapter: Jackson and "the Magic PJ's."

CHAPTER 2

JACKSON AND
"THE MAGIC PJ'S"

Michael Jackson wearing pajamas and slippers to court on the most critical day of the prosecution's case—when the young boy accuser finally took the stand—was one of the most masterful legal and media manipulations of all time. Those baby blue satin PJ's said absolutely everything the adolescent-like icon needed to convey to the jury and world: "I am just a harmless, rich celebrity, naively reliving my lost childhood."

Ironically, *USA Today* recently listed Jacko wearing the PJ's as one of the top ten "moments of *unscripted* behavior" in the past quarter century. Let's be clear, absolutely nothing about that day was "unscripted." I mean, come on, could anyone really believe it was some form of accident that Jackson wore PJ's to court on that critical day?

Perhaps Jacko was running late in hair and make-up and nobody in his wardrobe department noticed he forgot to put on his pants, along with the custom black sports coat with gold arm-bands and medallions. Even better, he ran late because he was waiting in line at the Santa Barbara ER that morning with back pain. *Please!*

Think about it. The PJ's silently screamed to the jury and world *Jackson's entire defense*: I am just a lost grown-up child who does not even know the difference between right and wrong courtroom attire, and I often engage in harmless conduct that most normal adults might construe as inappropriate.

Jackson and his lawyers managed to steal the entire trial away from the prosecutors and manipulate the worldwide media with one simple stunt.

There was no way Jackson's lawyer, Tom Mesereau, could have successfully argued that it's normal for a 44-year-old man to routinely invite young boys to sleep in their bed. The main defense was that Jackson is a unique icon who is *not* normal, but rather a harmless man/child reliving the lost innocence of his youth.

Jackson's lawyers managed to brilliantly display for the jury Jackson's childlike mindset, which would support their closing argument that basic rules of "normal" adult behavior are not applicable to "The King of Pop."

Instead of child molestation, everybody in the courtroom that day walked out primarily talking about Jackson's PJ's. In fact, that was really all anybody was talking about *after* that day, and it became the visual of the entire trial: Jackson getting out of his limousine with his umbrella-toting entourage wearing baby blue pajamas and slippers.

If Jackson had not worn PJ's to court, without question, the worldwide headline and lead story that day would have been: "YOUNG BOY TESTIFIES MICHAEL JACKSON SEXUALLY MOLESTED HIM," arguably the worst-case scenario for the pop star. Instead, most of the world's headlines were diverted to: "JACKSON SHOWS UP TO COURT IN PAJAMAS."

Jackson deflected what should have been the most triumphant day of the trial for the prosecutors, both inside and outside of the courtroom, virtually wiping out the horrific allegations from the media's profit-seeking coverage. The PJ stunt shoved the young boy's condemning testimony all the way to page 17 of most worldwide newspapers, when clearly it had been anticipated to be the front-page headline. Absolutely brilliant, but also absolutely detrimental to the name of justice!

The power of the PJ stunt can be demonstrated by how *little* of the boy's graphic testimony was reported in the news. Instead, what we saw on TV and in the papers were "experts" discussing Jackson's PJ's and frailty. Lost was the real news of that day: vivid details of how Jackson reassured the boy it was "totally natural, not to be scared," and "what they were doing was OK."

This young boy explicitly testified under oath that Jacko warned him that a man who doesn't masturbate could end up raping a girl, becoming disabled, or even having sex with a dog. That being said, the headlines from that day included:

"JACKSON ARRIVES LATE, WEARING PAJAMAS,"
and,

"PAJAMA DRAMA: HE'S LATE TO COURT, BUT DODGES JAIL TIME."

What was the downside to the PJ stunt? The jury and public might think Jackson was wacko? At that point, Jackson could have shown up with an elephant at his side and not have evoked any stronger feelings about his warped sense of reality!

No downside. Perfect upside. Legal genius!

What was particularly cunning about the PJ maneuver is I don't even think the media at large knew it was being manipulated—my point being confirmed by *USA Today* labeling Jackson's pajama stunt "unscripted." If the collective media machine *was* aware of the intentions behind it, the stunt was so grandiose that—even if clearly contrived—it could not have been ignored.

It was a legal maneuver that worked on almost every defense level, distracting both the jury and media circus from what should have been the worst day of Jackson's life. By contrast, if a non-celebrity defendant who was repeatedly accused of molesting young boys wore the same pajamas, slippers and face make-up to court, it is most likely his own defense counsel *would have stipulated to his guilt* just to expedite the process.

The PJ stunt showed how easy it is for the savvy to manipulate the media, and how successful they can be.

CHAPTER 3

THE "SLUMBER PARTY" DEFENSE

At the time of his trial, Jackson had been dealing with the media for almost 40 years, and was possibly the most profiled celebrity in modern pop culture. I have no doubt that, just as Jackson studied the history of Motown and other music legends, he also researched every possible option to avoid facing prison for child molestation.

It was clear from day one that Jackson's primary concern was to win the case outside the court in the media, hiring the then "it lawyer," Mark Geragos. Geragos was known for his experience in dealing with the media in the Winona Ryder and Scott Peterson cases, and had been a fixture on *Larry King Live* as a legal commentator. The hiring received mixed reviews, based on Geragos' concurrent handling of accused wife-killer Scott Peterson. It resulted in some bad press, which associated Jackson with the despised murderer.

When the opportunity arose for Jackson to get another "name brand" lawyer, he dumped Geragos and hired Thomas Mesereau. Mesereau was on a roll following his televised performance at the Blake preliminary hearing, which had resulted in Blake's release from jail after eleven months in solitary confinement awaiting trial. After becoming the new hot lawyer in America, Mesereau quit the Blake case to next work his magic for Jackson inside and outside the courtroom.

Mesereau had clearly learned from his experience with Blake, and again proved his ability by masterminding Jackson's winning trial defense. Together, they were unbeatable—the pajama stunt being the culmination of a calculated ploy to circumvent the gag order without Jackson having to take the stand.

I have personally gone up against Mesereau on the Blake case and I can tell you he is one of the best attorneys I have ever seen inside a court of law. Mesereau is a street fighter with a Harvard education, and is willing to do whatever it takes to win. Our dealings generated so much publicity together that I became the "go-to guy" for reporters and producers seeking negative sound bites against him. Despite our rocky history, which included Mesereau receiving severe sanctions from our judge, the worst thing I could ever say about him was:

"If I was ever in trouble, he is exactly the kind of attorney I would want representing me. But I am not so sure that is a compliment."

Tom Mesereau had several major problems heading into the Jackson trial. The first was trying to get around a gag order and reach the jury pool through the media. Mesereau desperately needed a way for Jackson to provide critical testimony to the jury without ever taking the stand for a cross-examination that most likely would have sent him to prison.

The second problem Mesereau faced was to justify Jackson "harmlessly" sleeping with 13-year-old boys. Let's face it; that simply is not normal, even for an oxygen-chamber-sleeping, "elephant man" collecting, eccentric pop star!

Jackson's legal team managed to come up with imaginative ways to accomplish their trial objectives, something I have dubbed: "The Slumber Party Defense."

We already covered the pajamas, but what else are things that people often associate with childhood sleepover parties?

1. PARTY INVITES
2. JUMPING ON THE BED
3. VISITS TO THE ER IF SICK OR HURT

To fully understand the brilliance behind the acquittal of Michael Jackson, all you need to do is cover the remaining elements normally associated with a childhood *pajama* sleepover party:

PARTY INVITES

You may not remember this, but it is absolutely true. Quite possibly a first in American jurisprudence history, on the day

Michael Jackson entered his formal plea of "not guilty" in court, he handed out invites to a party he was hosting afterwards.

While Jackson was facing the judge on seven counts of child molestation, he simultaneously had his assistants hand out invites to the hundreds of fans assembled at the courthouse. The actual invite to the post-molestation court hearing party at Neverland Ranch read as follows:

"In the spirit of love and togetherness Michael Jackson would like to invite his fans and supporters to his Neverland Ranch. Please join us January 16, 2004, from 11 a.m. to 2 p.m. Refreshments will be served. We'll see you there!"

It was reported on CNN that shortly before 2 p.m., traffic to the ranch was backed up more than two miles. One fan—or maybe lunatic is a better term—who attended Jackson's "not guilty plea to child molestation" party said it was a dream come true.

And you are going to tell me a state prosecutor should treat this matter like any other case? This is borderline twilight zone stuff—maybe Michael Jackson really is an alien from another planet who is completely oblivious to reality.

Jackson maybe, but his lawyers were far from clueless.

JUMPING ON THE BED

Much like he would do later with the pajama stunt, Jackson had also rewritten another worldwide headline on the day he was formally charged in court with criminal child molestation. Here is the CNN story headline from that pivotal day:

"SANTA MARIA, California (CNN)—Michael Jackson pleaded not guilty Friday to seven felony counts of child molestation, then went outside and climbed on the roof of his SUV, clapped his hands, stamped his feet and blew kisses to his frenzied fans massed outside the Santa Barbara County Courthouse."

OK, so he could not actually bring a bed to the courthouse parking lot! But come on, was not the identical visual created by climbing on top of his car in a party-like atmosphere? With music blasting and cameras rolling, Jackson jumped up and down on his black SUV, completely oblivious to its inappropriateness.

The visuals Jackson created for the mass media and watching jury pool, was of an eccentric rich icon, naïve enough to jump on his limo in the courthouse parking lot like an unsupervised child. *Perfect!*

Again, the dual objective was accomplished: invoking childhood memories of climbing where you weren't supposed to; and demonstrating the primary defense, "Jackson is just a big kid who does not even recognize what *others* perceive as inappropriate behavior."

While Jackson was still jumping up and down on the car, his then-lawyer was asked if the judge might be offended by Jackson's SUV stunt. He replied,

"He's Michael Jackson. He's an entertainer. He's not by profession a defendant in a criminal case. There is no rule book for how Michael Jackson, an entertainer, performs."

VISITS TO THE ER IF SICK OR HURT

First question: Have you ever heard of Jackson being spotted in an emergency room either before or after the trial? Michael Jackson does not go and stand in line for three hours at the ER for back pain or cold symptoms. *Not a chance!*

Can you picture Michael Jackson sitting in the packed ER waiting room, in a sequined navy admiral jacket, surrounded by sick people coughing and bleeding all around? As a general rule, people who employ "umbrella holders" do not wait in three-hour ER lines to see a tired intern with bad coffee breath.

Jackson is a man who would shut down entire malls in order to shop privately, but he was going to stand in line to fill out ER medical insurance forms? Let's see:

Name: Michael Jackson

Job: King of Pop

Prior Medical issues:

     Numerous nose and chin jobs

     Scalp burns during Pepsi commercial

     Extensive skin bleaching

     Pulled quad muscles from moonwalking

     Oxygen chamber overdose

Current Complaints:

     Cold symptoms

     Feeling run down during child molestation trial

     Lower back pain from sitting in court

Like a hurt child, Jackson made multiple highly publicized hospital runs during his trial. Precautionary emergency room runs are another visual associated with young children, exactly the role Jackson needed to play for an acquittal.

Dangerous criminals do not run to the ER when they don't feel well, and certainly don't wear satin PJ's to court after they are treated. I am sure Jackson and his team of stylists worked hard to decide which color pajama bottoms would make him look more innocent.

Baby blue turned out to be a good choice!

BASH THE VICTIM (OR MOM)

Jackson had an unbelievably difficult victim to discredit: a young boy who had suffered from cancer most of his life. It appeared as if he was unimpeachable.

However, Jackson and his lawyer, Tom Mesereau, hit the jackpot with the kid's parents—primarily his mother.

As soon as I heard on the radio that the kid's mom had previously sued JCPenney for false imprisonment and sexual assault, I knew Jackson would walk free. I had watched Jackson's lawyer, Mesereau, work on the Blake case, destroying witnesses at the preliminary hearing with far less ammo in his arsenal.

It was clear Jackson's conduit to freedom was through the young boy's mom. Jackson's pretrial media strategy was to leak information to the media about the mom, and present her to be the mastermind behind yet another attempt to rip off Michael Jackson.

It was indirect victim bashing. Or victim bashing one step removed. The message was a winner: blame the crazy, lying mom for everything!

As expected, Mesereau absolutely destroyed that mother on the witness stand. He drilled her on the large cash settlement she had won by suing JCPenney for sexual assault, and even got her to admit she had previously lied in court.

And then Mesereau hit a home run when it came to light that mom had been pampered at the spa at Jackson's expense. When Mesereau asked the boy's mom if she had received a "body wax" treatment from a spa, she strongly denied it under oath numerous times. Sensing a game-winning opportunity, Mesereau kept drilling her about getting a "body wax," to which she finally responded, "I had a *leg* wax done. He keeps saying 'body wax.' There is no body wax!"

Needless to say, she lost all credibility with the court, and, more importantly, with the jury.

Mesereau was clearly aware of the Spanish-speaking mom's language difficulties, and tweaked his questions to get a denial he could jump on. He threw himself a softball and then hit it out of the park. Also, because of Jackson's "fortune," the jurors were more inclined to see even a molestation victim's mom as a scammer because the jurors knew that winning the case meant a huge civil lawsuit.

The boy's mom was now seen as the villain, with Jackson as her potential victim. That was the ballgame!

That night, I am sure Jackson needed one less Ambien to get to sleep, washed down of course with his Diet Coke can filled with "Jesus juice."

CHAPTER 4

BLAKE'S TICKET ON
THE "LOVE BOAT"

Like Jackson, Blake was a person who studied high
profile cases, and he learned a lot from Cochran's
tactics on the O.J. case. Blake understood that he had power
over—and access to—his potential jury pool, and often
brainstormed how best to use it.

He brought in media consultants to discuss everything from
his courtroom attire to his hair color—opining grey was most
sympathetic. On jailhouse tapes made by hidden tape recorders,
Blake could be heard discussing some unbelievably revealing
information about his plans to win his case through the media.

Again, let's start with the basics facts of the Blake case, using
the same particulars, but a different name. You enter court and see
the defendant, RB: a longtime skinhead with a goatee, who is
covered with visible tattoos, and has dirty fingernails. The court
reads the following about the case:

*Defendant RB is charged with murdering his wife, a con artist
who trapped him with a baby that he will admit was "his worst
nightmare." Evidence will be presented that the defendant solicited four
separate longtime friends offering money to kill his wife.*

*Defendant RB claims to have simply left the victim alone in the
car for a few moments when she was killed. RB says he was "getting his*

gun" from the restaurant at the time she was killed. The car and murder weapon were found behind a dumpster down at the darkest part of the street. RB's wife was shot in the head through the open window in the passenger seat.

Defendant RB never called 911 for help despite having an available cell phone. The evidence will show RB instead walked back to the restaurant and sat in the lobby, requesting several glasses of water for himself after his wife was shot in the head. Defendant never requested to go to the hospital where she was later pronounced dead, and never asked about her condition.

Following the shooting, defendant RB's clothes were coated with gunshot residue, and particles were also found on his hands.

Six months before the murder, the victim filed kidnapping charges against defendant RB for stealing their baby. Defendant RB also had attempted to hire a retired LAPD officer to plant drugs on his wife in order to falsely send her away to prison so she would never get the baby back.

Two of the potential hit men had been friends with RB for over 30 years, and will tell you how the defendant offered to keep the door open to his wife's bedroom so she could be killed while sleeping. RB also helped map out an escape route the hired killer could take around the L.A. River.

Defendant only communicated with hit men using (what he believed) was an untraceable 30-digit calling card. His last calls to the hit men were the morning of the murder.

Defendant RB will not be testifying on his own behalf, invoking his Fifth Amendment right not to incriminate himself.

I mean, *come on*, this looks pretty bad for RB—don't you think? And I left a lot of details out of there, including admitting to a retired LAPD detective that he was going to have his wife "whacked."

Blake even contacted an ex mafia hit man in New Jersey.

Those are essentially the facts that were presented at the Blake murder trial and yet he beat all the charges made against him! He sat quiet, followed the O.J. plan, and walked free.

USING THE FIRST AMENDMENT, THEN TAKING THE FIFTH

One of Blake's first ideas for generating positive media coverage after his arrest for Bonny's murder, was a calculated plan to have "A-list" celebrities come to the L.A. County Jail for photo and press opportunities. Blake's plan was simple and potentially huge: to get as many A-list celebrities as he could to come down to the L.A. County Jail to visit him, in the hope that the potential jurors would be affected by Hollywood star power.

"It should be one person after the other. You call another one and say, 'Would you come to the courthouse with us one time…and afterward go out and talk to the public?'"

With the enthusiasm of a person planning a birthday party, Blake brainstormed names of celebrities he could use in his jury-tainting plan: "John Travolta. Big, big fan," Blake told his publicist during a jailhouse visit in 2002. "A real important fan…. World-class fan."

The staged party list of possible invitations continued. Fearing he could only get B-list stars to come and visit him in jail, Blake devised a plan to get "one huge star" to show up and open the floodgates.

"My first bet is going to be Sean Penn. He could be the one!" Blake also stated, "Alec Baldwin is a big fan. He actually sent me fan letters…I'd put him up with Sean Penn as one of the heavyweights that might be the one to start the ball rolling and make some calls."

Blake then shifted to another A-list person to help taint his jury pool: Kevin Costner. "Kevin Costner comes up to me and says, '*Baretta*. I never could get enough of it. I watched it….' I must not have written his name down. He and Alec Baldwin are big timers. He's perfect!"

The names kept flying, "Marty Landau, Burt Reynolds, Tony Bennett would come to see me, his son is a friend…I know Tony would come…." But the problem Blake had was a lack of A-list connections: "I think we can forget Sean Penn because he and Brando are best friends."

Not to be deterred, Blake switched gears to the next level and discussed the B-list potential. Longevity in the public's eye was key according to Blake, who suggested somebody like Bob Newhart's TV wife, Suzanne Pleshette: "The whole world loves her."

Blake didn't even care if he knew the celebrity or not. Friendship was clearly not the issue, as illustrated by his instructions on how to call "Mrs. Newhart."

BLAKE: Hey Suzie, I want you to do me a favor. I want you to come and visit Robert one time, and tell the world what you see. Would you do that for—just that little—and if it's not Susie, it's another Susie. It's—who's that girl that played the bionic woman?

VISITOR: Linda—Linda

BLAKE: No

VISITOR: No, no, no, Wagner.

BLAKE: Lands. Lindsay Wagner.

VISITOR: Lindsay Wagner.

BLAKE: Somebody like that. In other words, somebody like me. Somebody that's been around a long time….

VISITOR: I will. Susie is a good idea. I will call Susie.

BLAKE: Uh, uh, uh who's Rickle's best friend?

VISITOR: I have no idea.

BLAKE: That comic that worked with Susie for 20 years, for 30 years. Ask him.

VISITOR: Oh, Bob Newhart.

BLAKE: Bob Newhart. Gavin MacLeod.

VISITOR: All right.

BLAKE: Gavin MacLeod is perfect.

VISITOR: Is Newhart a friend of yours?

BLAKE: Yeah.

VISITOR: All Right.

Close friend, huh!

Blake was clearly digging deep into his 70s bag of tricks, making a pitch for *The Bionic Woman* herself, Lindsay Wagner, to help with his media defense. Finally, Blake went for a money player, Gavin MacLeod, the beloved captain of *The Love Boat*.

At first, Blake was not interested when former 70s pin-up star Scott Baio's name popped up. Clearly not impressed with the *Happy Days* and *Charles in Charge* actor, Blake initially dismissed talk of Baio's visiting with: "Tell him to send me a letter."

It would later become apparent that Blake did not have the juice to glamorize the jailhouse visitors' sign-in sheet he anticipated. Even the B-list actors Blake hoped to fall back upon had no interest in the publicity stunt. The *L.A. Times* contacted Lindsay Wagner when this jailhouse tape story broke, and she told them she had no involvement.

With no real hits on his celebrity fishing rod, Blake later appeared to lower his standards, asking his agent on the phone, "Is Scott Baio coming down?"

At one point Blake had the idea to have bumper stickers made that said, "FREE ROBERT BLAKE." The idea was to have them distributed throughout the "Valley" areas, where the jury pool for the murder trial would be selected. Blake discussed the plan with a friend during a jailhouse visit.

"There's some bumper stickers out there called 'Free Robert Blake.' ...And I'm just thinking maybe you and Mort and Dale, we can come up with some sort of plan to get them made. I don't know where the hell you distribute them, or you put them in stores and have people sell them, or what the hell you do with them.... Go through the Valley."

Like a local politician, Blake talked about targeting the specific neighborhoods his jury pool would be selected from. "That's a great idea. We got to start distributing them in the San Fernando Valley." He even considered what TV shows his potential jury pool would watch, realizing the power certain shows have to create a buzz within the industry.

Larry King's interview program is a good example. When Blake commented that nobody in the Valley watched Larry King, he was advised of the importance of *Larry King Live* to springboard new stories on a national scale. Blake realized that a good hit on King's show would be reported by other news outlets, many reaching his jury's home in the Valley.

Blake then began brainstorming how to get favorable publicity on *Larry King Live* by using his and Bonny's daughter, Rosie (my client in the estate), to gain sympathy. "I will get on the phone and talk to Rosie and Larry King will have a hook-up so that everybody in America can hear me talk to Rosie," Blake said, in a jailhouse police transcript. "If I do well, it'll be a radio spot on every radio in America for a year."

Blake was a master entertainer, and knew how much buzz he could generate if he nailed his lines. But he also warned, "Don't let it look like a performance."

While in jail, Blake coordinated photographs taken of him with his new grey hair and jail uniform, ordering his attorney's office to "have a couple hundred copies made…give it to everybody." He would use his new older look to generate undisputed sympathy, making sure the images were distributed "all over the fucking planet."

Blake was involved in every aspect of his media campaign for acquittal. He was even upset when his then-lawyer Harland Braun did an interview with the *Today Show* host, Katie Couric, stating Diane Sawyer would have been better.

Not surprisingly, Blake had kind words for anyone in the media who was favorable in their reporting. He was clearly thrilled with his choice of TV interviewer, Barbara Walters, rewarding her with exclusives before and after his trial. He also loved the Associated Press' longtime reporter Linda Deutsch, stating she was "terrific," but "nobody reads newspapers."

MY WIFE HAD IT COMING

I often said to the media that I did not believe Blake's lawyers invented victim bashing, but they took it to a new low. Blake essentially had his lawyers sell the theory that his dead wife was a totally bad person and deserved what she got.

That first year after the murder, Blake's high-priced legal team devoted itself exclusively to the public trashing of Bonny Lee Bakley in the press. The murder victim became a media villain while Blake remained free of charge.

I remember seeing a picture in the paper of Blake holding up their baby girl reaching over Bonny's casket at the televised funeral—very dramatic. And, in my opinion, very staged.

Blake's lawyers had completely vilified the baby girl's mother, calling her "evil," a "con artist," "gold digger," "celebrity stalker," and "grifter," barely concealing their obvious point: *she had it coming!*

For almost a full year, the Los Angeles D.A.'s office allowed Blake's lawyers an unopposed free reign over the mass media. The result was the potential jury pool along with the rest of America knowing way more about Bonny's mail order business than the extensive evidence against Blake.

All the trash talking and "Bonny bashing" came exclusively from Blake's lawyers, never Blake himself. This was a thin yet surprisingly strong layer of insulation to distance Blake from the outrageous slander campaign against his murdered wife.

An example of early seed planting by Blake's lawyers was their falsely telling the media that somebody had been stalking Blake's wife, and she had asked Blake to carry a gun for her protection. Braun told the media:

"Our investigators are now searching the house after the LAPD finished…. With our assistance, there may be stuff in her property that could provide clues…. The police didn't really have a chance to understand her background, so there may be a clue that we can find that they didn't…. The problem is that she had sort of a checkered background, [being involved in a] lonely-hearts con scheme [in which she conned lonely men out of money through ads across the country]. She claimed that she stopped it."

By far the biggest job I had after taking the Robert Blake wrongful death case in 2002 was trying to level the playing field after Blake's highly effective media production. Braun avoided me at all costs in the press. I recall a time that he threatened to cancel his appearances on CNN if I was involved in the segment. Never once would he debate me on the case—I would have loved that! I guess Braun was having much more success attacking Bonny and her family without anyone to oppose his rhetoric, which makes perfect sense—allowing me to participate might actually have shed some truth to the matters being discussed.

Even years later on, I remember doing CNN one morning on Paula Zahn's show and stating how Blake had kidnapped the baby from Bonny and then planted drugs on her in Arkansas in order to falsely send her to prison. After my segment, the two co-hosts looked at each other on-air and said they had never heard any of that before and point-blank questioned the accuracy of my statements.

This was two years after the murder, and CNN, along with the rest of America, knew very little about the true facts of the case. Obviously the Bakley children needed somebody to stop the public attacks. Blake and his lawyers' free reign in the media was about to end, and I would be the one to end it.

My only real criticism of the Blake prosecution was I believe they allowed all the pretrial negative publicity about Bonny to alter their case. To me, it seemed like the Blake prosecutors traded a victim for a motive, and almost stipulated that Bonny was a horrible person to explain why Blake needed her dead to protect their baby.

The end result was identical to what the defense wanted from the very beginning: to have the jury care more about Robert Blake than the loss of the victim.

I actually got a media assist from O.J. alumni Marcia Clark early on in the case, commenting on Braun's media conduct. Marcia Clark told Fox TV she did not believe Robert Blake was convincing as an innocent man, blaming, in part, his lawyer Harland Braun's ongoing smear campaign.

"In my humble and constitutionally protected opinion, Robert Blake looks like the guilty party.... Whenever I see a smear campaign on the victim, I think: desperation time."

When the time finally came for me to take Blake's deposition and talk about the real facts of the crime, his lawyers brought a motion for a belated gag order on the case. Here is the actual press release I sent out—evidently upset by my opposition's attempt to cling onto the uneven playing field they had so carefully set up.

"RE: ROBERT BLAKE WRONGFUL DEATH 4-21-05 HEARING /GAG ORDER REQUEST

"The children of Bonny Lee Bakley find it absolutely appalling and grossly unfair for the Blake lawyers to now claim a need for a gag order after spending four years bashing the murder victim with outrageous lies and half-truths. It is no surprise the announcement comes a few weeks before Robert Blake's deposition as an obvious attempt to block the public from hearing about the true facts of the murder.

"Robert Blake and his team of lawyers have spent four years intentionally tainting the jury pool about Bonny and her family. In fact, Robert Blake recently bragged how he spent millions on lawyers and investigators digging up dirt ultimately never used at trial, but only to trash his wife to the press.

"Robert Blake and Earle Caldwell have done extensive media since the verdict, and both defense lawyers even did press conferences today immediately after, raising this issue. Any attempt to gag Robert Blake and Earle Caldwell's involvement in the murder is in bad faith and should be flatly denied—as it was before.

"After four years of victim bashing against Bonny and her family, the children and the American public have the right to learn about the true facts of this case, not just the misinformation leaked by the Blake lawyers to create the impression Bonny deserved to die. Robert Blake must answer all questions about the plotting and murder of his wife at the upcoming May 9, 2005 court-set deposition. Plaintiff counsel will be ready."

BASH THE POLICE

The microscopic spotlight placed on the LAPD in these high profile cases is extreme. After some bad press, LAPD Chief Parks had decided to allow a former *L.A. Times* writer full access into the elite Robbery and Homicide Department for a year to do research for a tell-all book. The detectives were not thrilled, but had no choice.

During the cross-examination of various police departments, it was frustrating for everyone when the defense strategically dwelled on the mistakes that had been made. In Blake's trial, there were a couple of zingers that Mesereau milked for all they were worth—I must say, very effectively. His biggest punch was the fact that a book author had been allowed full access to the crime scene on the night of the murder.

Now, the author had been riding with the homicide detectives for a full year before the Bakley murder ever happened, mandated by the chief of police to show the public they had nothing to hide. However, Mesereau was able to spin it that the detectives themselves were seeking fame, and an author roaming free at the crime scene felt wrong.

It was near the end of the one-year deal when the Bakley murder occurred and, just as he had done with all the other cases, the author, Miles Corwin, was allowed to tag along to the crime scene and later to Blake's house. When the book finally came out, Blake was only a small chapter towards the end—more than enough for Tom Mesereau to drive a truck through during the preliminary hearing!

Mesereau put up numerous pictures from the crime scene showing homicide detectives huddled in the dark night examining various clues. With a detective on the stand, Mesereau pointed to a man in the middle of every picture and asked, "Now who is this person walking freely around a secured crime scene?"

"That's book author Miles Corwin."

Mesereau made it seem like the detectives had hired an author to document their rise to fame, when they were just following orders. You could almost hear a collective gasp from the packed courtroom, with everybody thinking, *How could the police chief let him tag along like that? Did he not learn from O.J.?*

Obviously, the fact that an author was walking around the crime scene played into Blake's defense of the fame-seeking police needing "a big one" post O.J. Furthermore, in celebrity/high profile cases, mistakes by the police do not look like mistakes—they look intentional.

An example of an inflated claim of police "misconduct" hammered at the Blake trials involved the murder weapon, which was found in a dumpster next to Blake's parked car. The gun was found with a loaded bullet in the chamber, and the police ejected the bullet so the gun could be safely transported to the station.

The argument Blake's lawyers made was the detective should have tried to catch the ejected bullet midair with a baggy, and not have let the bullet hit the ground. The point? The LAPD was trying to destroy potential fingerprints, just in case they did not later turn out to be Blake's. Blake's lawyers argued that the LAPD had already made up its mind against Blake, and therefore could not risk the existence of physical evidence that would contradict their theory.

The simple truth was the police do not transport guns that still have bullets in the chamber. Safety is their number one priority. Police officers safely disarm weapons, they do not try to eject and catch deadly bullets like a center fielder would catch a lazy pop fly. This is the same reason they did not empty out the dumpster where the murder weapon was found in the middle of the residential street, as Blake's lawyers argued they should have. It was safer for the families and children that lived there for the detectives to first move the dumpster to an empty field.

The other big trumped-up point made against the LAPD in the Blake case was a typo contained in a search warrant, where a detective wrote ".25 auto" instead of "25 auto," when copying the content of a to-do list found in Blake's handyman, Earle Caldwell's truck. Blake's lawyers had numerous blow-ups of this clerical mistake, and flat out made it seem like the detective had doctored the evidence.

Not even close to true, but the truth often took a back seat.

When the time came for the jury trial, Blake's new lawyer, Gerald Schwartzbach, simply followed Mesereau's blueprint from the preliminary hearing all the way home. Even though Schwartzbach could not match Mesereau by way of trial skills, Mesereau's script was so detailed it was just a matter of memorizing the lines and hitting the marks.

CHAPTER 5

PHIL SPECTOR AND THE "ACCIDENTAL SUICIDE"

Spector falls more under the rich than famous umbrella; a reclusive, behind the scenes record producer who worked with some of the greatest musicians of our times. In fact, the 911 operator who took the call on the night of the shooting at his mansion clearly had no clue who Phil Spector even was, responding, "Who? Seal inspector?"

Spector met the beautiful actress/victim Lana Clarkson late at night while out at a bar, and apparently worked enough charisma to convince her to take a limo back to his mansion for a tour. She was found dead near his front door, shot in the face, with her purse slung over her shoulder on a chair.

It would turn out that numerous women would later come forward and state that Spector had pulled guns on *them* in the past when they tried to leave without his permission.

The pretrial taint of the jury pool was probably more important to Phil Spector than the others. The Spector lawyers actually *created* a new defense term I have never heard of before his murder case. With virtually no other angle to play, the sole defense for Spector was that this beautiful blond actress committed "accidental suicide."

Accidental suicide?

Now, many would agree I am not an English scholar, but aren't "accident" and "suicide" conflicting terms by definition? A person can intentionally die by committing suicide, or unintentionally die by accident. Right?

Was Spector's lawyer saying she only meant to shoot herself point blank in the face, but accidentally died in the process?

Wow!

A difficult argument, even if their client did *not* have an extensive history for pointing guns in women's faces.

In the opening argument, NY superstar lawyer, Bruce Cutler, (John Gotti's lawyer) told the L.A. Spector jury this was an "accidental suicide." The defense was that this beautiful woman, out of the blue, shot her face off with Spector's gun on her way out of his house that evening.

So again, let's walk through the celebrity formula to freedom, applying it to the facts of the Spector case. You are called for jury duty and find out in court the following information about defendant PS:

Defendant 65-year-old PS is charged with shooting a beautiful 40-year-old woman in the face as she tried to leave his house in the late hours, after they met in a bar earlier that night. The woman was found dead by the defendant's front door, purse slung over her shoulder, allegedly attempting to leave after refusing the defendant's sexual advances. The defendant walked out with blood and gunshot residue on his hands and told his limo driver, "I think I just killed someone."

The defendant never called 911 for help, and tried to wipe the blood off himself and the dead victim before the police arrived.

Five other women will come forward and tell you about when they had also rejected the defendant's sexual advances and he had in turn placed a gun to their faces.

The defendant will not be taking the stand on his own behalf, taking the Fifth Amendment right to not incriminate himself.

Let's be serious! He was all alone with the beautiful woman in his house, she was shot in the face with his gun trying to leave, and he *confessed*, "I think I killed somebody."

That's a tough sell, even with the best defense lawyers in the world—*for a non-celebrity.*

A key witness in the Spector case was Spector's limo driver who was waiting outside to take Lana Clarkson home. While waiting in Spector's black Mercedes, he heard a "pow" sound, and said about a minute later, he saw a bloody Spector emerge at the doorway holding the gun.

He then called 911 after Spector apparently told him, "I think I killed somebody."

And that's exactly what the prosecution argued it was—a full-on confession. Spector's attorney, Bruce Cutler, however, attempted to completely dismiss this devastating evidence of guilt as "five words allegedly said to someone taking a siesta."

In a feverish pitch, Spector's defense team attacked the driver's English skills, energy level, and immigration status, in order to prove reasonable doubt.

Specifically, Spector's lawyers said he was "a substitute driver with a language problem, who was full of snacks and cookies and water and sound asleep, sitting in a closed car, with the heat on, and the radio on, and the fountain going."

Now we have two truly innovative defenses working: the "accidental suicide" and "the Chips Ahoy" defense!

I must admit, I have had a lot of cookies in my day, but I have never been delirious enough in a chocolate frenzy to confuse a statement like, "I think I killed somebody," with "this crazy blond just 'accidentally' blew her face off with a gun, get help now."

It turns out the limo driver attended private schools in Brazil and earned his BS degree before coming to the U.S. on a student visa to study English. During the trial, he spoke clearly and reportedly had no trouble understanding what was asked of him.

However, his English slipped a few times as he referred to Spector as "she" and called a briefcase a "wallet."

Does that equal reasonable doubt and trump a point-blank confession?

USE THE FIRST/TAKE THE FIFTH

Spector tried a few different things to follow the Michael Jackson eccentric celebrity defense, attempting his own PJ stunt in the form of an outrageous Afro haircut and high-heel pumps. Unlike Jackson, "seal inspector" showing up to court in a mega Afro wig and platform shoes only made him look creepy *and* guilty.

Fortunately, somebody on his defense team got a hold of him and stopped that nonsense quickly. By the time trial rolled along, he had clearly been worked over by a PR firm, wearing toned down outfits with a short blond haircut.

On the creepy scale, he went from a "9" to a "6."

Next, Spector pulled out his celebrity access pass to the media, and gave an interview to *Esquire* magazine—which was then circulated worldwide before his murder trial began. Spector conveyed his entire testimony of events to the jury pool, without having to face any cross-examination from the prosecution.

Use the First. Take the Fifth!

Spector's unchallenged pretrial testimony was that the victim, Lana Clarkson, "kissed the gun" before shooting herself. Spector said, "I have no idea why…. I never knew her; never even saw her before that night. I have no idea who she was or what her agenda was."

Spector even claimed he did not know where she got the gun from! At trial, the answer was revealed: *him*. The murder weapon came from Spector's gun holster, which he kept in a drawer by the front door to his mansion.

Maybe Clarkson was snooping around in the hope of finding a gun to *accidentally kill* herself.

Spector also told *Esquire* Clarkson was "loud and drunk" before they left the House of Blues club in Hollywood, where she worked as a hostess.

"She asked me for a ride home. Then she wanted to see the castle…. She grabbed a bottle of tequila from the bar to take with her. I was not drunk. I wasn't drunk at all. There is no case. She killed herself…. It's 'Anatomy of a Frame-Up'…I didn't do anything wrong…. This is not Bobby Blake. This is not the Menendez brothers. They have no case. If they had a case, I'd be sitting in jail right now."

Through this self-serving statement, Spector used the media to hit several of the standard celebrity defense prongs: victim bashing, describing her as both drunk and suicidal; and LAPD bashing, bringing up visions of O.J. and a police "frame-up."

In the *Esquire* article, Spector insisted that he was "innocent" and claimed to have called the police *himself* that night.

Actually, I think he was wrong on *both accounts*.

ATTACK THE VICTIM

Phil Spector faced a similar obstacle Robert Blake had faced with regards to his reputation. Numerous women came forward claiming Spector had also threatened them with guns before when they tried to leave his "castle." There were years of rumors about him pulling out guns in recording studios, even in the presence of John Lennon and other legends.

Joan Rivers' former security guard testified he twice had to eject a gun-toting Spector from parties, with a dejected Spector screaming that all women "should be shot in the head."

While Blake clearly had more ammunition to attack his victim, Bonny Lee Bakley, in his defense strategy, Spector's investigators ended up finding a document to support the suicide defense. Some of Lana Clarkson's diary passages revealed her visions of seeing a washed-up actress who killed herself with a gun.

Furthermore, the victim's diary recorded her fascination with guns, feelings of depression over her failing acting career, and struggles with alcohol and drugs. Some entries found in the victim's computer reportedly talked of suicide, violence and lack of hope.

Not only did this diary support the primary defense, it also cast a major shadow on the prosecution's credibility because it was withheld from the coroner who had ruled out suicide because of how hopeful the victim appeared. The coroner had testified the only information he was given about Clarkson convinced him she had no tendency toward suicide, creating the appearance to the jury that critical information had been concealed from the coroner before reaching his opinion.

Huge!

As a trial lawyer, if you are going to have your critical expert witness (the L.A. coroner) go the extra mile and say this lady was *not* suicidal, would you not expect the victim's diary to be used by the defense lawyers as an infallible impeachment? Once again, the ghost of O.J. popped its ugly head into the courtroom, and the question of "how far would the prosecution go for a big conviction?" was underlined in the juror's notepads.

In addition, there were e-mails sent to a friend by the victim in which she said she was despairing over financial problems and even feared becoming homeless. In a vague reference, the victim stated that she was considering getting her affairs in order so she could "chuck it."

Less dramatic entries include sections of the diary where she described waking up in the morning, brushing her teeth, eating cereal, shopping for apples, and returning home to wait for *Deal or No Deal* to come on TV.

Not exactly expecting the keys to the Kingdom anytime soon, but suicidal?

Spector's lawyers argued the victim's writing showed she was delusional. He claimed that the prosecution's withholding of the information from the coroner was strong impeachment, and "weakens and shakes his opinion." The defense argued:

"She's seeing people who are deceased and talks to them. She talks about seeing a dead actress who comes to her in visions, a struggling actress who didn't make it and killed herself with a gun."

On the flip side, the prosecution claimed that the writings were unauthenticated and maybe fictional. They tried to downplay the material, stating the writings were unreliable and were probably done for a creative writing class the victim had been taking.

The trouble with this argument was that the title of the writings found on the victim's computer was "The Story of My Life."

The initial gravity of the problem for the prosecution became clear when Judge Fidler responded to the prosecution's argument for withholding the writings from the coroner.

"I think you are arguing way too much. If you have the words of a deceased...how do you keep that away from the jury and away from an expert who could have considered it?"

Things were looking bad. Pre-production was gearing up for O.J. part IV.

However, as often happens in trials, momentum can change in a flash. After the judge took the writings and e-mails home to read in their entirety, a dramatic change of judicial opinion occurred. Judge Fidler was "clearly peeved" when he returned to the bench and *rejected* the introduction of the victim's manuscript.

The judge indicated that the victim's manuscript was so different from what the defense had represented, he actually had to check to see if he had the right document. "I don't consider anything in this particular document to be significant. I find nothing of any probative value whatsoever in this item."

The judge did end up allowing Spector's lawyers to cross-examine the coroner on the writings, despite being upset about the overreaching representations. In response, the prosecutor took the coroner through the various e-mails cited by the defense, reading the full messages, trying to show that the defense's interpretation of suicide was wrong.

"Is there any suicidal ideation?"

"No," the coroner replied.

Obviously, the coroner had not changed his opinion that it was murder. Still, the damage was done, and the defense had laid the foundation for a few power punches needed for their closing argument.

SPECTOR JUDGE SAYS LEAVE HER ALONE

In a refreshing ruling, the judge on the Spector case openly put the kibosh on the defense's plans to bash the victim during trial. He could not stop the information from being leaked to the media, but impressively he put his foot down in court.

A first in modern high profile justice.

The issue was prostitution, and the media leaked allegations of the victim's past. In the middle of the trial, it was widely reported that the victim, Lana Clarkson, had worked for a Hollywood madam—maybe as a call girl—at some point in her life.

The *L.A. Times* ran a huge article about how the defense "might" call Clarkson's alleged ex-employer madam, and she "might" testify about these allegations of prostitution. The jurors becoming tainted by this information once the story became so glaringly public, was almost guaranteed.

The judge promptly took action, and mid-trial held a hearing away from the jury on whether the Hollywood madam could testify. Judge Fidler stated, "It appears to me that she's there to dirty up Miss Clarkson…. You certainly can show me otherwise that there is some valid basis for her testifying."

Spector's lawyers denied the obvious attempt to victim bash, telling the judge that it was "not our intent to trash Miss Clarkson. What is our intent is to give the jury as much of what was going on in Miss Clarkson's life."

Request denied, and their madam was banned from testifying.

BLAME THE POLICE

Spector's lawyer, Bruce Cutler, implied that the LAPD was using Spector as a scapegoat to compensate for the humiliating O.J. loss, repeatedly and angrily blaming the LAPD of making a rush to judgment. Spector's lawyers followed the standard blueprint, and argued that any mistakes made by the police were intentional in order to get a conviction.

And, of course, the usual mistakes were also there. For example, the coroner testifying in Phil Spector's murder trial acknowledged there were crime lab mistakes in the collection and handling of evidence, including moving the victim's body, which compromised the crime scene. He also testified that the LAPD criminalist lost a piece of the victim's tooth.

The missing tooth fragment was among other concerns with the case listed in an in-house coroner's office memo. The memo also said the LAPD criminalist wrongly used "lift-off tape" on the victim's dress and ultimately compromised the investigators' ability to evaluate blood spatter evidence on the dress.

Furthermore, the coroner testified the victim's body was mistakenly moved during the police investigation, causing blood to flow from her mouth. Again, he directly accused the police of compromising critical evidence and jeopardizing the evaluation of the blood spatter on the victim's dress.

The coroner also admitted he could not tell who was holding the gun when it was shot. "There are two ways to look at it, the person could have been holding a weapon at the time of discharge or could be in the vicinity."

But the real issue of the Spector case investigation had nothing to do with the LAPD, but rather Spector's star expert witness, Dr. Henry Lee. It was suspected that he was responsible for a missing piece of critical evidence.

THE "CSI EFFECT" AND O.J.'S STICKY-FINGERED EXPERT

When it came to lawyers and defense experts, Spector wasted no time lining up the remnants of the O.J. "Dream Team." First, Spector hired Robert Shapiro for a reported one-million-dollar retainer, and then brought in famed expert witness, and fellow O.J. "dream team" alum, Henry Lee.

Henry Lee was a former chief criminalist from Connecticut, and escalated to high profile fame after the 1995 O.J. Simpson murder trial. In fact, several Simpson jurors cited Lee's trial testimony in their decision to acquit Simpson of the murders.

Lee would become a focus in the Spector trial as well; his participation generated one huge question that hovered over the entire trial: Did the famous defense expert steal and destroy critical, incriminating evidence from the crime scene?

Like a dramatic storyline on a TV show, a former Spector attorney came forward saying she saw Henry Lee pick up what appeared to be an acrylic fingernail fragment in the foyer area, during the investigation of the house on the evening after the murder.

She testified that she saw Lee put "a little white thing" in a vial and remove it from Spector's house. Her testimony was backed up by a former defense investigator, and retired sheriff, working with Spector's then-defense attorney Robert Shapiro at the scene that day, saying the object looked like a gunshot-stained nail.

Prosecutors were contending that if a piece of Clarkson's nail snapped off during a tussle with Spector, it would defuse the defense's claim that she "accidentally shot" herself. L.A. prosecutor, Pat Dixon, Blake alum, immediately argued that the white object Lee pocketed was the victim Lana Clarkson's acrylic fingernail, which would show that Clarkson's hand was in front of her face when she was shot and that "her hands and her fingers were not on the trigger."

Lee said he was "astonished and insulted" by the accusations by the two former members of Spector's defense team, stating, "I think my reputation [is] severely damaged."

In a dramatic ruling, the judge began by calling Lee a "world-renowned expert." However, ultimately he believed the former lawyer, and that Lee did take evidence from the crime scene. Judge Fidler stated, "If I have to choose between the two, I am going to choose Ms. Caplan is more credible than Dr. Lee.... Dr. Lee has a lot to lose if this turns out to be true."

Judge Fidler ruled, "Dr. Lee did recover an item that was flat, white and irregular around the edges." Fidler said he couldn't say whether the item was a fingernail, but he ruled that jurors could be told about the missing item and decide for themselves.

In response to the ruling, Lee released a press statement to the *L.A. Times* and numerous outlets, calling the fingernail controversy a "slanderous attack" and "a tactic to kill the messenger before the message is delivered."

Right on point, a spokeswoman for the district attorney, said of Lee's statement: "Whatever he says should be said under oath on the witness stand."

Lee never showed up in court again and the defense never put him on the stand for the jury. However, Spector had a handful full of *other* experts who could easily fill in for Lee. Several defense experts opined it was suicide, using extensive data to indicate almost all gun in mouth shootings are suicides. Furthermore, several high-end experts testified that blood splatter on Spector appeared to have traveled six feet, making it impossible for him to have pulled the trigger himself.

Of course, the prosecution had experts to counter that Spector *could have* been close enough to pull the trigger, but when it comes to the game of "reasonable doubt" the tie goes to the defendant!

Even the opinion-for-hire argument did not go very far for the prosecutors, and in fact backfired. When Spector's blood expert was being drilled on cross-examination about getting paid for his opinion, he responded, "I have plenty of money, it is time I don't have." The jury laughed, and that is never good when trying to get a murder conviction.

Towards the end of the trial, the prosecutors were sucker punched by the Spector lawyer's intentional violation of the rules of trial. It was conduct disturbingly reminiscent to what had previously resulted in the disbarment of the D.A. handling the Duke lacrosse team case earlier the same year. Spector's lawyers had withheld critical information about defense expert Michael Baden's trial opinions. Baden is a world famous forensic pathologist, often featured on HBO, hired by Spector to support the suicide theory. Not only was Baden a top expert in his field, he was also married to one of Spector's lead trial lawyers handling the case.

In a complete shock to the prosecutors, Baden testified at trial that Clarkson did not die instantly, and lived long enough to have coughed the condemning blood onto Spector's clothes. This was a bombshell new theory, which had never been mentioned to the D.A. during the two-year mandatory pre-trial exchange of evidence. Baden claimed he had had a revelation the Sunday prior to taking the stand, and had never shared the new theory with any of Spector's lawyers—*not even his wife.*

The prosecutors were livid, and, after clearing the court of the jurors, Judge Fidler "scolded" Spector's lawyers, accusing them of a "deliberate and egregious" violation of discovery rules. The judge stated: "There was a violation. It was to gain a tactical advantage and to throw the prosecution off their game," noting for the record the prior discovery violations by the defense. Judge Fidler threatened strong punishment for the defense conduct, stating: "It's the only way we will put an end to this game playing."

As harsh as this exchange may sound for team Spector, *the jury saw none of it!* Even though the Judge would later tell the jury about the misconduct, Spector still reaped all the benefits of the surprise testimony surely supporting reasonable doubt!

Baden was paid $110,000 for his work on the case. I don't know if he got any additional money for his "new" expert revelation.

CHAPTER 6

SCOTT PETERSON AND THE BOGUS "STAR CHIPS"

Scott Peterson was never famous for anything *other* than killing his beautiful wife just as she was about to give birth to their first child. Although he committed the most heinous crime conceivable, his good looks promoted him to magazine poster boy status, all the way up until his conviction.

Across America, there are around a dozen weekly "entertainment" magazines, ranging from *People* to *The National Enquirer*, and if there is a current celebrity trial, it is guaranteed to make the cover. I was told that Scott Peterson sold more magazines for *People* than any other person featured on its cover in 2005. For consecutive weeks, either he or his beautiful late wife, Laci, featured on almost every magazine and paper cover across America.

However, just because you have done something *infamous* does not mean you have the type of fame that lets you get away with murder. This was the trap door that Scott Peterson and Mark Geragos blindly walked into and it was a long hard fall!

Scott Peterson was not a beloved celebrity. Jurors did not look over at the lawyer table and see *Baretta* or #32, they saw a smug punk who killed a woman and baby—*his baby*!

I know it must seem like I am beating up Geragos, but the truth is the few times I have met him, he was a really nice guy. He is funny, has a star quality about him, and I am sure overall he is a fine lawyer.

However, I must say my mouth absolutely hit the floor when he promised the Peterson jury he would prove Scott Peterson "stone cold innocent." This was a titanic mistake on two major counts:

1. Never make a promise in your opening you can't keep.
2. Never take away the "beyond a reasonable doubt" burden of proof the prosecutors are obligated to meet.

In my opinion, Geragos did both.

In his opening, he also made an empty promise to the jury to present witnesses who would show Laci Peterson was kidnapped by a satanic cult. That never happened and he left the jury hanging in disappointment.

It was as if Geragos had forgotten high profile trials are about winning the game of "reasonable doubt." One of the main reasons the celebrity trial formula works is the "reasonable doubt" burden is unfairly elevated, and virtually impossible for a prosecutor to meet.

There has not been a single case, from O.J.'s to Blake's, where the objective at trial was to show the defendant was innocent—never mind "stone cold innocent."

I mean, *hello?*

If you ask the majority of the jurors on the Simpson, Blake, or Jackson cases whether they felt the defendants were even "luke warm innocent," they would probably say *no.* What the jurors have said in these cases is that the prosecutors did not meet their burden of proof that the defendant committed the crime "beyond a reasonable doubt." Big difference!

Geragos volunteered to accept the burden of proving Peterson innocent and virtually relieved the prosecutors of their obligations.

Another low point for Geragos involved his expert witness on the issue of Laci's pregnancy. This "fertility" expert was supposed to testify that Laci's unborn son lived beyond the time prosecutors contend Peterson killed her. The intention was to show the jury Peterson could not have been the killer under the prosecutor's timeline.

Unbelievably, during cross-examination, Geragos' high-priced expert conceded to the jury that he may have been "mistaken" in his expert testimony and opinions.

Shortly after that fiasco, Geragos rested the defense presentation without delivering on the critical promises of his opening. No satanic cult, no unsavory transients, and no "stone cold" innocence.

It was clearly a bad decision not to put Peterson on the stand. Without any real fame chips, the jury would not allow him to hide behind the Fifth Amendment. The jury members saw a murderer, and got nothing from the defense to change their minds. Geragos seemed to be playing the celebrity hand without knowing he did not have the cards to win.

After the trial, one of the jurors said, "We were on the edge waiting for this big defense lawyer to show us who kidnapped Laci and [the] people who saw her alive on the morning she vanished and [was] being pulled into [a] van. But there was nothing."

Another juror added, "I looked over at the defense table and it looked as if they felt, '*Shit, we fucked up.*' "

And finally, this comment which is possibly the worst insult Geragos could have received from a Peterson juror: "He had all these lines at the beginning, even though he didn't have to prove anything. There were no scientific experts who could back his arguments.... As a juror, I wondered, maybe he ran out of money for the case."

Geragos also sent a negative message by not sticking around while the jury deliberated. In fact, he did not even make it back in time for the reading of the verdict itself. Geragos was in Los Angeles, and did not give himself enough time to fly back for the reading of the death penalty verdict against his client.

He watched it from home on CNN.

CHAPTER 7

A MEDIA STRATEGY—
EVEN BEFORE THE CRIME

Both the Michael Jackson and Robert Blake criminal trials had one major thing in common: their victims were used in their primary defense both inside and outside the courtroom.

The accuser's mother was the most tangible confirmation of "reasonable doubt" Jackson had to offer up to both the media and the jury. Jackson surely knew she had previously sued JCPenney for sexual assault and had settled with them for a nice chunk of change.

Jackson had also provided his accuser's mom with trips to a spa, while he was alone with her kids. Privacy aside, did Jackson deliberately create activities for her, in order to set up reasons for impeachment later down the line? Did he know she could then easily be discredited if it were ever necessary?

Of course he did, and it worked!

In Robert Blake's case, there is disturbing evidence that he had designed his murder defense campaign, even before he killed his wife. There is physical evidence that could reasonably lead one to this conclusion—a tape.

This dramatic revelation occurred at the Los Angeles police station, only a few hours after Bonny's murder. Blake had just completed tape-recording an evasive statement for the detectives.

After the interview, the homicide detectives left Blake and his longtime civil lawyer, Barry Felson, alone in the room. Unknown to both of them, the recording device located within the walls was *still on* as they began to talk privately between themselves. The exact conversation whispered between Blake and his longtime lawyer went as follows:

FELSON: We better call Harland first thing in the morning to make sure this goes the way it is supposed to.

BLAKE: Do you have the tapes ready to go?

FELSON: No, but we have the transcripts.

Let me pose a few questions: Blake was told his wife had died at the hospital just minutes prior to the recording, so why had he already hired a criminal lawyer to defend him? What tapes/transcripts did they prepare before the murder and have "ready to go"? Why were they both *already* on a first name basis with criminal defense lawyer, "Harland" Braun?

And most significantly, what did Felson mean by: "make sure this goes the way it is supposed to"?

The attorney/client privilege will most likely keep these answers concealed forever.

CHAPTER 8

PRISON BREAK STAR
VS. DUKE D.A. DISBARMENT

Two recent cases making national news demonstrate apparent differences in the rules the state prosecutors and high profile defense lawyers play by when dealing with the media.

The rules of ethics are supposed to govern all equally. However, the recent disbarment of the Durham County District Attorney, partially resulting from his media conduct in the Duke lacrosse rape scandal, no doubt sent a shiver down the spines of prosecutors around the country.

The Duke case was a huge media sensation, and was also the first high profile case to define the ramifications of overstepping the grey line between ethics and media spin. Two separate categories of conduct led to the permanent disbarment of the Duke case D.A. Mike Nifong:

- Pretrial comments made to the media during the investigation of the Duke case; and
- Failure to turn over test results to the defense in a timely manner.

In recent California cases, the defense has been able to easily get away with similar conduct unscathed. A perfect example can be found again with Harland Braun, this time representing a young actor who was involved in a deadly drunk driving crash.

A few years after the Blake case, a young star of the hot TV show *Prison Break* was behind the wheel during a fatal drunk driving crash, which killed a teenager in his car, and severely injured two others. The TV star hired Harland Braun after his arrest, and Braun wasted no time working his highly questionable media rhetoric.

A comparison of the media comments made by Braun with the comments made by the Duke prosecutor—resulting in disbarment—demonstrate the extreme contrast of consequences.

1. PRISON BREAK MESS

In 2007, an actor from the TV show *Prison Break*, Lane Garrison, was involved in a fatal car accident while allegedly drunk driving. It was reported that Garrison had met three teenage fans of *Prison Break* while in line at a grocery store on a Saturday night, and accepted their invitation to join them at a party. The crash occurred at some point during the party, when they all got into Garrison's car.

Shortly after the accident, Garrison hired former Blake lawyer Harland Braun as his defense counsel. Much like he did on the Blake case, Braun went right to the media with a bunch of irresponsible statements, without any real concern for the actual truth.

And of course, Braun targeted the most important legal publication of our time—*TV Guide*! Here is the story:

"BREAKING NEWS: Prison Break Vet's Real-life Tragedy

Prison Break's Lane Garrison hadn't even planned on going out that Saturday night he crashed his car into a tree, killing a 17-year-old boy. But when three teenager fans in the checkout line of a grocery store invited him to a party, he couldn't resist. 'He didn't even know their names,' Garrison's lawyer Harland Braun tells *TV Guide*. 'It was a casual encounter. He was an actor accommodating some fans.'"

For starters, what a dreadful spin for Braun to describe this fatal accident as "an actor accommodating fans." But, Braun did not stop there, and clearly did not let the true facts obstruct his *TV Guide* quotes:

"While Braun says Garrison was 'naïve' not to realize he was out with minors after local curfew, he insists his client doesn't have an alcohol problem and doubts drinking was the cause of the accident."

Braun actually told *TV Guide* that he *doubted* the accident was alcohol related. Here is an idea: How about asking your client for answers before going public with statements?

The *TV Guide* article came complete with a picture of the accused actor crying in front of a church, with a caption saying how concerned he was for the victim's parents. A pretty good score for Braun considering *TV Guide* can be found in virtually every grocery store checkout line in America.

Oh, but it gets so much shoddier.

Braun also went to the popular new website *TMZ*, founded by the producer of the defunct TV show *Celebrity Justice*, Harvey Levin. *TMZ* had become extremely popular after breaking the Mel Gibson drunk driving/Jew tantrum story, and was often one of the links on the AOL welcome screen.

Here is the *TMZ* spin that was given to them by Braun:

"TMZ has learned that *Prison Break* star Lane Garrison has hired powerhouse defense attorney Harland Braun in connection with last Saturday's fatal car accident.

"Lane was at the wheel in his Land Rover on Saturday night when it crossed a median in Beverly Hills and crashed into a tree. A 17-year-old boy sitting in the backseat was killed and two 15-year-olds were injured.

"Braun tells *TMZ* that Garrison had never met the three teenagers before the night of the accident. Braun says Garrison was at a local supermarket earlier in the evening when the trio recognized him in the checkout line and asked him if he wanted to go to a party.

"Braun says Garrison went to the party and had one drink. Braun says Garrison also had one margarita at a Mexican restaurant that night, but that was the extent of his alcohol consumption.

"Braun tells *TMZ* that as Garrison was leaving the party to meet a woman at his apartment, the three teens asked to accompany him. According to sources, the boy was an only child and was extremely well liked by his peers. Braun says Garrison has no recollection of the accident, which Braun says rendered him unconscious. In fact, Braun claims Garrison's first memory was waking up at the Century City Hospital emergency room with a taxi coupon on his lap that had been given to him by hospital staff so he could get home.

"Braun says he was not told by hospital personnel that someone had died. He learned of the death later from a friend, Braun says, and was 'totally despondent.' Braun says a sample of Garrison's blood was taken at the hospital, but it could take several weeks before the results are in.

"Braun says he doubts Garrison was intoxicated, but also says, 'Who knows if someone put something in his drink at the party.'

"Braun also says Garrison's Land Rover had been experiencing alignment issues as of late and had been pulling to one side, and added that the SUV had brake problems. Braun says he is forwarding repair receipts to the police. According to Braun, 'Nobody knows what happened, it's a mystery.'"

Let's just break down some of the unbelievable statements Braun made to *TMZ*. These statements would prove not only to be false, but dangerously close to complete misrepresentations:

- Garrison only had one drink at dinner that night: a margarita at a Mexican restaurant. He doubts Garrison was intoxicated.
- Maybe somebody put something in his drink at the party.
- His car had brake problems.
- Garrison was leaving the party to meet a woman at his apartment, and the three teens asked to accompany him.
- Nobody knows what happened, it's a mystery.

Well guess what ended up happening?

Lane Garrison pleaded *guilty* to all charges.

It was reported later that, not only did the *Prison Break* star slam numerous shots of vodka at the party, he actually *brought* a bottle of Grey Goose Vodka to the minor-filled party, offering shots to kids while partying himself. When the booze started running low, Garrison agreed to make a liquor run to supply more alcohol to the party.

The three teenagers went with him, and the fatal crash ensued.

The Beverly Hills police reported that the young actor had over a .20 blood alcohol level, along with cocaine in his system at the time of the fatal crash. I have read that in order to have a .20 blood alcohol level a 200-pound person needs to consume 12 drinks in three hours (two full bottles of wine).

What was Harland Braun's response?

"Police shouldn't discuss evidence publicly."

Braun decried the police department for publicly announcing the blood alcohol lab results, stating it was "a totally irresponsible thing," to do and that it "was basically a public trial...designed to influence potential jurors." Braun complained to the *L.A. Times* that the police were "trying the case in the press," stating:

"The real question now is, 'Can you get a fair trial when the police chief and all these police men have already put out this version?'"

Truly unbelievable!

2. THE DUKE SCANDAL

Now, let's compare the statements made by Harland Braun in his representation of the *Prison Break* drunk driving case with media conduct of the now-disbarred D.A. in the Duke case.

In March 2006, a scandal rocked Duke University when the local D.A. Mike Nifong publicly accused several Duke lacrosse players of raping a girl hired to "dance" at their party. Until then, Duke had been a rock star in the world of college athletics, primarily because of its acclaimed basketball program and coach.

The scandal ultimately caused the cancellation of the entire season of Duke's championship-caliber Lacrosse team, and even the firing of the coach who had nothing to do with the ordeal.

Unlike the high profile defense lawyer who typically seeks fame and fortune through one dramatic victory, the Duke prosecutor Mike Nifong had spent 30 years working towards being elected County D.A. At the time of the Duke incident, he was facing a tough fight for re-election to keep his coveted job.

When the media showed up in Durham and offered him the red carpet to national attention, he grabbed it in hopes of boosting his name brand. It may have looked like the road to legal glory, but in fact it was a one-way ticket to national disgrace, resignation, and disbarment.

Unfortunately for Nifong, when the masses of cameras started rolling at the worldwide press conferences, he left his ethics script in the locker room toilet. Despite 30 years of public service, Nifong got lost in the spotlight of the surreal media circus—and then just got lost period!

Some of the media sound bites that would end his career included referring to the Duke lacrosse players as "a bunch of hooligans," and stating his own personal opinion that he was "convinced there was a rape."

Nifong was also charged by the Bar for wondering out loud "why one needs an attorney if one was not charged and not doing anything wrong." He also speculated that the accused players could have been wearing condoms preventing any DNA link from the players to the rape accuser, despite the victim telling him no condoms were involved.

Nifong later said he regretted stating he wouldn't allow Durham to become known for "a bunch of lacrosse players from

Duke raping a black girl." In his media frenzy, he went to the extreme of telling reporters the alleged crime was spurred by a "deep racial motivation."

He later conceded to the state bar, "I think that I crossed the line," and maybe got "carried away a little bit" when talking publicly about the case.

It turns out the girl was lying, and changed her version of the events. Furthermore, the D.A. withheld critical DNA evidence from the defense lawyers that later cleared the accused boys of the crime, even lying to the court himself, on several occasions.

Nifong's excuse for failing to turn over the DNA results may have been the lamest of all time, saying he was "too busy campaigning for re-election to his D.A. office," was facing "an unprecedented number of challengers," and "was not always able to give his full attention to the case."

The truth was Nifong had withheld the exonerating DNA results for six months, finally turning it over to defense lawyers just a few days before the election he ended up winning. He milked all the media attention until he won the election, and then dropped the rape charges based upon the DNA evidence he had concealed.

Nifong tried to justify his comments by saying he lacked the media or political savvy to know when he crossed the line. He also said, "certainly what I was trying to do was to re-assure the community, to encourage people with information to come forward."

I completely agree that the D.A. must be held to the highest standards of ethics when it comes to criminal prosecution. In fact, our entire criminal judicial system is designed to allow 100 guilty people go free rather than one innocent person go to prison. There is no question that nobody would ever want themself or a loved one to be falsely charged with a horrific crime like rape.

But that being said, crime victims also have a right to justice, and defense lawyers should be held to the same ethical standards.

Nifong was charged by the North Carolina Bar for making misleading and inflammatory comments to the media about the athletes under suspicion, violating the rules of professional conduct. Specifically, he was accused of making "improper commentary about the character, credibility, and reputation of the accused," with forty-one separate quotes cited in the Bar's complaint.

In deciding to disbar Nifong based solely on his conduct on the Duke case, the State Bar stated:

"Well, what we have here, it seems, is that we had a prosecutor who was faced with a very unusual situation in which the confluence of his self-interest collided with a very volatile mix of race, sex and class, a situation that if it were a plot of a John Grisham novel it would be considered to be perhaps too contrived. At that time he was facing a primary and yes he was politically naïve. But we can draw no other conclusion than that those initial statements that he made were to forward his political ambitions. But having once done that and having seen the facts as he hoped they would be, in his mind the facts remained that way in the face of developing evidence that that was not in fact the case."

The Bar opinion further stated:

"You can't do justice in the media; you can't do justice on sound bites. The way to arrive at a determination of the facts is to hear in a fair and open proceeding all of the evidence and then for the trier of fact to determine what the facts are…. This is also a case where due to the initial strong statements, unequivocal statements, made by Mr. Nifong, there was a deception perpetrated upon the public. And many people were made to look foolish because they simply accepted that if this prosecutor said it was true, it must be true."

At some point early in the Duke case, *Newsweek* magazine figured out what the D.A. was doing, and planned to blow the story wide open. In a rare look behind the scenes, the following are actual e-mails exchanged between the *Newsweek* reporter and Nifong before the worldwide story broke:

From: Susannah.Meadows
To: Michael.b.Nifong
Sent: Tuesday, 13 June 2006 2:46pm ET
Subject: Possible cover story
Dear Mike,

I've been going over these documents in the duke rape case. And I have to tell you that they raise questions about what was known while you were making certain assertions. Please can we talk about this. I'm not asking that you comment on anything that isn't public. We're getting ready to do a big story about this, possibly on the cover, about how certain things were said in public when the facts were known to be different. We won't close the issue until Saturday morning. Please think about commenting. As it appears now, it doesn't look good. But I'm sure that's because we haven't heard your side. I can be reached at_____. I'll be in Durham tomorrow night through Friday. All the best, Susannah Meadows

From: Michael.B.Nifong
To: Susannah.Meadows
Sent: Tuesday, 13 June 2006 4:25pm ET
Subject: RE: Possible cover story
Ms. Meadows,

I am afraid that I must decline your request for an interview. All of my public comments in this case were made prior to any specific defendant being identified, and were essentially restricted to 1 (my belief that the victim had in fact been sexually assaulted) and 2 my hope that one or more of the persons who were present but not involved with that assault would cooperate with the investigation.

Once specific defendants were identified, I considered myself to be ethically bound to avoid any further comments on the case or the evidence. That has left the field pretty much open to the defense attorneys. That part I understand, and have no choice but to live with. What has surprised me is the utter lack of any degree of skepticism on the part of the national media with respect to the claims of the defense attorneys, many of which are misleading and some of which are absolutely false.

As an example, when those attorneys held press conferences to announce that the first round of DNA testing "completely exonerated" the players (a claim that, on its face, is rather preposterous). I saw not one single report that any reporter had actually seen the results (none of them had) or had asked to see them and had that request denied (which is what happened to those who bothered to ask).

Now you are going over "documents" in that case. Where did you get them? What other documents did they not show you? But, of course, you cannot possibly know. Is anyone surprised that the defense attorneys are spinning this case in such a way that things do not look good for the prosecution? Their job, after all, is to create reasonable doubt, a task made all the easier by an uncritical national press corps desperate for any reportable detail, regardless of its veracity. Did not exactly the same thing happen with the Michael Peterson case in 2003? Do you recall how that one came out at trial?

Now, to get specific, what are you accusing me of saying in public "when the facts were known to be different?" None of the "facts" I know at this time, indeed, none of the evidence I have seen from any source, has changed the opinion that I expressed initially. I have seen quite a bit of media speculation (and it is even worse on the blogs) that either starts from a faulty premise or builds to a demonstrably false conclusion. That is not my fault (although some of your colleagues have acted as if it were).

The only people I have to persuade will be twelve sitting on the jury and if you want to know how I am going to do that, you will need to attend the trial. If, in the meantime, you and other "journalists" want to continue your speculations in the competition to come up with the most sellable story—and that seems to be everyone's bottom line—then please spare me the recriminations when you get things wrong, as you inevitably will.

Not that this will make the slightest bit of difference to you, but the real irony of this whole situation from my point of view is 1) that my initial cooperation with the press was based not on any perceived political advantage to be had, but on my (in retrospect, admittedly naïve) belief that such cooperation would help effectuate a more accurate public discourse on an issue with great societal resonance; 2) that my initial comments on the situation before there was a case against any identified defendant which would trigger the ethical rules resulted in my being accused of unethical behavior, and now my silence, which is mandated by those ethical rules, is apparently raising further speculation about the ethicality of my behavior; and 3) the lesson I have learned from all of this is that I would probably be best served in the future by avoiding speaking to the press at all.

Mike N

The rest is history, much like Nifong's license to practice law!

CHAPTER 9

HIGH PROFILE
HALL OF FAME

CELEBRITY LAWYERS

One of the ancillary bonuses of the O.J. saga was that it opened the door to trial lawyers becoming celebrities— reality TV personalities evolving well outside the limited box of Court TV. Cable news stations jumped on the bandwagon, and now many of the hosts you see are trial lawyers gone Hollywood: Greta Van Susteren, Dan Abrams and Nancy Grace, to name a few.

Think about how many lawyers' names you knew before O.J.'s dream team, outside of Clarence Darrow and Perry Mason. O.J.'s case started the trend, making household names out of Johnnie Cochran, Marcia Clark, Robert Shapiro, Barry Scheck, Daniel Petrocelli, Christopher Darden, F. Lee Bailey....

I mean what even qualified Marcia Clark to become the "legal correspondent" for *Entertainment Tonight*? Losing a huge trial watched by the world? The key word is being "watched." It really is true that no publicity is bad publicity (OK, almost true). Christopher Darden became a "legal expert" for CNN—why? Was he not universally panned for his losing performance in the O.J. case, best known for the glove fiasco?

Even Mark Fuhrman became a commentator for Fox News, and I won't even write down the word that made him a household name.

The perfect example of the no-publicity-is-bad-publicity philosophy is Mark Geragos. Let's be honest, Geragos has lost virtually every big trial he has been in, exactly like the 1970s Minnesota Vikings of the legal world. He lost Winona, got fired from the Michael Jackson case, and then lost Peterson.

Even though Geragos *lost* all these cases, he lost them all over the pages of *People* magazine! The end result: Does anybody know or remember the name of the prosecutor who *won* the Peterson trial? How about the name of the attorney who convicted Winona Ryder?

Exactly!

However, Geragos should have left behind his L.A. attitude before heading to Modesto County in Northern California, where the Peterson trial took place. In my opinion, walking in and out of court in $300 sunglasses, $2000 suits and always being on a cell phone might not have sent the best message to the small community. Geragos was acting like a rock star, but could not win over his audience of 12.

Everyday of the Blake trial, I had cameramen and reporters follow me from the parking lot until I entered the front door of the courthouse. Almost always, two or three jury members would be outside sitting on the front bench watching the action.

I was *always* conscious of this dynamic, and would modestly say hello to all the media people, never talk about the case, and never break my stride to the building. I was respectful and professional, careful not to be a diva about it.

While the best defense lawyers have mastered the art form, the State's top prosecutors have fatally remained frozen in the losing philosophy that "the case will be treated the same as every other case." Even worse is the stale quote, "We will not try this case in the media."

That is ridiculous!

Like it or not, with or without you on board, the case *is* being tried in the media, and the jury pool is listening.

The majority of high profile trials take two years or more to finally pick a jury and go to court. What that means is both sides have two years to speak to the prospective juries through the media, and the winner of public opinion has an outright advantage before the trial ever begins.

Even more potent, the lawyers can say virtually anything they want in the media without any rules of court or guidelines to monitor their conduct. Lawyers can basically testify for their clients to the media, and never have to explain their comments to the jury.

At the beginning of every trial, the judge instructs the jury "what a lawyer says is *not evidence*," evidence can only come from the witness stand. The exact opposite is true in the media where *everything* a lawyer says about their case is valued as evidence—true, false, or irrelevant.

Believe me, every single trial would be much easier if you were allowed to say anything you wanted to the jury before the strict evidentiary rules kicked in.

THE WRONG REASONS

Geragos also lost playing the celebrity hand in the Winona Ryder shoplifting trial. Geragos curiously turned down all plea bargains and rolled the dice for a reputation-making, high profile jury trial. Ryder was charged with shoplifting from Saks Fifth Avenue, in an apparent attempt to keep her clothing budget under $10,000 a month.

The first major problem Geragos had in defending Ryder against the shoplifting charges was the prosecution had a video of Ryder stealing the subject merchandise. The second major problem was *the prosecution had a video of Ryder stealing the subject merchandise.*

What in the world was Geragos thinking going to trial, when *they had her on tape?*

Look, as warped as the celebrity justice system is, O.J., Jackson, and Blake would all be cellmates at San Quentin's death row if any of them had been filmed mid-crime.

Why in the world would you go to trial on the Winona Ryder case, turning down a slap on the wrist plea bargain, knowing your client *did* help herself to a "five finger discount"?

The answer is both sad and simple: there is very little camera time in a closed-door settlement.

Did Mark Geragos *really* think he could convince a jury to ignore the videotape of her cutting off sensors and bagging the merchandise? Was it really in his client's best interest to become the poster child for shoplifting, or rather to make it go away quickly and quietly?

Or did Geragos know the simple truth: it did not matter if he won or lost as long as he got his name in front of the media?

In fairness to Geragos, both sides of the Winona Ryder case got caught up in the media glare and tried to make that case something it never should have been. Not too many people in middle America lost sleep over an overpriced hat from Saks Fifth Avenue on Rodeo Drive. Most people think big celebrities get their clothes for free anyway.

Maybe both sides should have waited for Winona to escalate her game to knocking off banks!

Following the story of Winona Ryder from jail, even Robert Blake was puzzled by the media attention the actress was stealing from him. "Marcia Clark, she beats me up everyday. Who's Geragos? Winona Ryder, why is it such a federal case?"

QUEEN GLORIA

When I first met Gloria Allred in New York City at the *Today Show*, she was comforting Peterson's mistress, Amber Fry. Fry was wearing a green dress, and was embarrassed for not realizing it was St. Patrick's Day.

Gloria told me she represented Blake's first wife, Sandra Blake, and asked if I wanted to take her deposition. Sandra had been married to Blake for 20 years and was the mother of his two children, but she had always refused to discuss Blake publicly.

Of course I said yes!

The setting for the dramatic deposition was Gloria Allred's office in Los Angeles. On the way over, Gloria called me on my cell phone to discuss how to best handle Sandra, failing to mention a surprise that was waiting for me in her lobby.

I went up her building elevator to her floor, and as the door opened, Gloria was curiously standing there ready to greet me. I said hello, stepped out of the elevator to shake her hand, and noticed she had the entire media circus lined up in her lobby ready to film our greeting!

I had no clue they were waiting in her office, and literally looked like a deer in the headlights when they showed the "summit-like" entrance on the news that night. A "heads up" would certainly have been nice—something along the lines of, "Hey Eric, I have the worldwide media filming the elevator, make sure your fly is not down."

Not her style.

We went into the conference room, and Gloria left to get Sandra for another staged media entrance. In the meantime, Blake walked into the large conference room alone, and sat down a few seats across from where Sandra would be testifying.

Remember, Sandra had never confronted Blake nor discussed the rumored horrors of their marriage in over 20 years, and now she was about to do it on camera under penalty of perjury—with Blake staring her down from across the table seven feet away.

Tense is an understatement!

A few moments later, Sandra Blake walked in with Gloria, avoiding any eye contact with Blake. Sandra sat next to Gloria on one side of the table, directly opposite from me, Blake and Ezzell.

The court reporter at the head of the table swore her in.

Sandra began crying as she detailed both the physical and emotional abuse she had endured throughout their 20-year marriage. It was riveting! She was strong and brave as she choked back tears to tell story after story, ranging from Blake shooting a gun at her, to his plan to have her former boyfriend killed.

In the middle of recalling a violent fight she had with Blake, Sandra all of a sudden turned her head and began speaking directly to Blake. "He grabbed me, got on top of me, started slugging me with your fists. Robert, I know you know."

As I left the conference room for our first break, I was shaken to the bone over what I had heard. I made my way down a long hallway to get my composure back, and I looked up to see Blake heading toward me, obstructing my path. As we awkwardly approached each other, he gave me a big wink and smile as if it were a sunny day at the beach.

It sent chills down my spine!

A few months later, I got a call from Gloria's assistant saying that they would not be making Sandra available to testify at my trial. It did not matter because the judge had already ruled her testimony inadmissible. However, my impression was that after Gloria got the media time she wanted, helping my clients get justice became obsolete.

The next time I saw Gloria was at a TV studio in L.A. I had gotten there early, and was hanging out in jeans and a t-shirt. Gloria arrived in a limo, and walked right by me as I said hello. A few minutes later I changed into my suit, and she finally looked at me long enough to realize who I was, paying me the courtesy of a "oh, hello Eric!"

In all fairness to Gloria, the cameras were not yet rolling.

DON'T BILL FOR HUBBY'S DRY CLEANING

The short but bright flame of Anna Nicole Smith's death, and the subsequent televised court fights, shed light on a full spectrum of high profile trials' worst traits. Who could forget the Bronx-born, presiding Florida judge that often took over the questioning of witnesses due to his obvious lack of faith in the lawyers' abilities (maybe he wasn't wrong there)?

He comically addressed the lawyers in court by the names of their home states, saying things like, "You Texas," or "California, what's your objection?" There were dozens of lawyers, all making the rounds on every single TV show that would have them.

The hearings may have been in Florida, but everything going on had a Hollywood feel. In fact, it appears that everybody who was exposed to the extreme media attention in the Anna Nicole Smith hearings *completely lost their minds.*

The judge made a dramatic and tearful reading of the verdict on live TV, ruling that Smith should be buried with her son in the Bahamas. A few weeks later, the same judge left his 25-year judicial career to parlay his notoriety into a permanent TV career. It was reported CBS gave him a pilot based on his *performance* during the Smith hearings.

It was also reported that the original Florida judge, who passed on the Smith case, was later caught smoking a joint in a public park filled with children. Maybe he and "Judge Florida" could do a Cheech and Chong remake together.

But above all, one participant always stood out to me as an extreme spotlight seeker: Larry Birkhead's lawyer, Debra Opri. Maybe this falls under the category of takes one to know one, but watching the coverage, I noticed she always seemed to be wearing brand new clothes and wedging herself into every possible camera angle—standing just a little too close to her client to make sure her new Armani suit made the shot.

On one occasion on the L.A. news, they showed her at a press conference, standing behind Stern's lawyer, heckling him while he spoke at the mike. It was almost like a weigh-in for a professional boxing match as the two lawyers bickered at the podium in front of the media.

My speculative opinions were confirmed a few weeks into the charade when Larry Birkhead reportedly fired Debra Opri for the exact reason of enjoying the spotlight too much. Ms. Opri did not take kindly to this, and went on the TV show *Extra*, saying, "I just had enough…I can't represent a client who has a middle man by the name of Howard K. Stern. I feel very comfortable in my decision, and I wish Larry the best. But I am worried about him."

Opri implied she had quit, as opposed to being fired, saying, "I don't want anyone to think that I'm jumping ship. He's close enough. He's getting the DNA results today in the Bahamas. I didn't abandon Larry."

But the fun did not stop there! It was next reported on the *TMZ* Website that she had billed Birkhead an amazing $620,492.84 for her legal fees and costs. It was reported that her charges included:

- $96,068 in cell phone charges.
- $4,500 for Opri's personal publicist.
- $119 per e-mail (minimum).
- $4,265 for cell phone roaming charges in the Bahamas.
- $14,000.00 for "preparation for and attendance" at Smith's televised funeral, reportedly attending against Birkhead's wishes.
- $1000-$2400 dinners.

Opri even felt justified in billing her client $25.75 for her husband's laundry, when he decided to tag along on the Bahamas trip.

In total, it was reported to be a 112-page bill. Opri reportedly offered Birkhead the discounted rate of *only* $511,365.09—on the condition he accepted it immediately. Opri wrote, "I'm still willing to accept the discounted billing at this time, but only without further discussion."

What a sport!

Birkhead claimed Opri had said she was willing to represent him free of charge, because "the publicity from her representation of Plaintiff would greatly benefit Opri's legal career." Birkhead further alleged that Opri had placed her own career desires and needs above his, and had falsely represented herself as a specialist in California family law. A fraud lawsuit followed, and the State Bar investigated as well.

Larry Birkhead later went on *Larry King Live* and compared Opri to the demonic character from the *Nightmare on Elm Street* movies. "It's kind of like one of those Freddy Krueger movies when you try to get rid of somebody and they keep coming back."

Opri's "publicist" later told *TMZ*, "Debra Opri always gets paid. That's what she does for a living."

Curiously, around the time of their public fighting, Birkhead wound up on the cover of *Globe* magazine holding his newly awarded baby girl, with the headline reading: "IS LARRY AN UNFIT DAD?"

Inside, the story ran a color picture of Birkhead and Opri, noting the two "are now at each other's throats." The article cited several allegations by Opri, indicating Birkhead's bachelor apartment was so "filthy" it needed to be cleaned by a professional maid service as well as baby-proofed before the baby's arrival.

Birkhead claimed Opri would often leak information to the media, and then privately ask the reporters to question her about the information, only to refuse to comment once she was on the air.

Nice touch. Even Gloria would be proud of that one!

A few months following the Birkhead fight, Debra Opri was representing David Hasselhoff's wife, Pamela Bach, in her custody battle with the *Baywatch* star. Shortly thereafter, a horrible videotape surfaced all over America, showing an inebriated Hasselhoff eating a Wendy's hamburger while his daughter videotaped his drunken stupor and pleaded with him to quit drinking.

As a result, Hasselhoff temporarily lost visitation rights to see his kids. However, a few weeks later the tables turned when he was granted "sole physical custody" of their daughters, leaving Opri and her client to suffer defeat.

After losing custody, it was reported that Bach was overheard fighting with Opri, yelling, "I just lost my kids!" Bach then fired Opri, making it the second time in a matter of months the attorney had been dumped from a high profile case.

David Hasselhoff's lawyers then filed a motion in Superior Court to obtain Opri's financial records, to determine whether she received money for the sale of the infamous video to the media. They claimed she made hundreds of thousands of dollars for leaking the daughter's private tape to the press.

DON'T MESS WITH MAN'S BEST FRIEND

The recent case of football superstar Michael Vick demonstrated two points. First, the media's power to condemn an accused, even before charges are filed, is growing stronger. The horrific pictures of Vick's dog torture compound were plastered on every paper in America, and Vick's corporate sponsors were pulling out—even before the police were pulling in! Vick pled guilty, and then held a massive press conference for damage control. No trial, no jury, just a media firestorm and a simple guilty plea!

The second lesson from the Vick case is: don't mess with animals, especially with dogs! America can apparently look away when it comes to most celebrity crimes or indiscretions, but we have our limits!

We will see if Vick's athletic talents can overcome his grave wrongdoings. After all, Kobe Bryant received a clean slate after his Colorado mess was dropped, but, then again, he never admitted guilt.

PARIS BURNS L.A.

"It's so cruel what has happened to her," the friend told *OK!* magazine. "She wasn't allowed to wax or use a moisturizer. Her skin is so dry right now!"—Hilton's friend after Paris was released, having done three days out of the original 45-day sentence. Excerpted from the *NY Post.*

I was recently at a deposition in Orange County, California, and in the common hallway they had big TVs mounted on the walls. During a break, I looked up to watch *MSNBC LIVE* talking about Paris Hilton's early release from jail, and whether problems with her *hair extensions* was the reason she was set free.

MSNBC is talking about Paris Hilton's hair extension problems, and we are still at war in Iraq?

I was actually embarrassed, not for anybody in particular, just embarrassed. It was like CNN following Michael Jackson's commute to court with live helicopter coverage, with updates like: "Jackson has just turned left into some form of parking structure." What is "newsworthy" is often defined by what generates viewers!

I am not saying Lindsay Lohan or Paris Hilton don't matter, I am just saying they don't matter any more than you or me! It was an insult to our troops to devote full-day coverage to focus on Paris Hilton and her gourmet cupcake delivery.

It reminded me of a clip Howard Stern always plays, of a news TV show doing live coverage of a post 9/11 event, when the reporter stopped mid-story and interrupted with breaking news: I'm so sorry to interrupt the story but I have just been handed breaking news. BEN AFFLECK AND J-LO HAVE BROKEN UP.

In a town of never-ending high profile surprises, we got a few twists and turns with the Paris Hilton fiasco.

It started like a simple Hollywood fluff story. Famous-for-being-famous tabloid fixture, Paris Hilton, was ordered to serve 45 days of jail time for violating the terms of her probation from an alcohol-related reckless driving case. It appeared like just another story from 2007, blending in with a number of other Hollywood stars having some troubles like Britney Spears, Nicole Richie and Lindsay Lohan.

Hilton was sentenced to 45 days in jail—a month and a half in jail for driving with a suspended license! The judge expressly prohibited home confinement. I mean think about it, a month and a half in jail with some of the most hardcore criminals on the planet for driving with a suspended license?

By comparison, on the same day Hilton got 45 days, a woman was sentenced to about 120 days for shooting her husband in the back until he was dead. Another woman received an identical 45-day sentence for molesting a young boy student at a YMCA cabin, the boy attending the school where her husband was the principal.

After California governor Arnold Schwarzenegger refused a requested pardon by Hilton, Hilton decided to accept her punishment. First she went to the MTV Movie Awards, and then to jail (at least she skipped the after parties).

Shortly thereafter, L.A. Sheriff Lee Baca informed the media that Hilton's sentence was being slashed to 23 days from the 45, awarding her good-time credit *even before she had started her sentence.*

Next, Sheriff Baca unilaterally let Paris go free after four days, sending her home to finish her sentence on house arrest with an ankle bracelet—*against the express orders of the judge.* Sheriff Baca cited a medical reason, but never actually bothered to produce the paperwork in an almost defiant gesture against what he saw as a resource-draining charade.

People across the country flipped out, even Reverend Al Sharpton from New York managed to make national headlines on the topic. Sharpton said the early release "gives all of the appearances of economic and racial favoritism that is constantly cited by poor people and people of color…. I think that it's both another glaring display of how race and money seem to get different treatments. There seems to be a different criminal justice system for some than others."

The story of her early release even sparked headlines in two major New York papers, "BLOND JUSTICE" in the *Post* and "THROW HER BACK IN JAIL" in the *Daily News*.

Los Angeles city attorney, Rocky Delgadillo, could not resist the pull of the worldwide media attention, and became the spokesperson against Hilton's early release. He started throwing media punches everywhere, primarily at L.A. Sheriff Baca for letting Hilton out early.

"We cannot tolerate a two-tiered jail system where the rich and powerful receive special treatment.... I have directed my criminal branch to immediately explore all possible legal options to ensure that the law is being applied equally and justly in this case."

Delgadillo even filed a contempt of court motion against Sheriff Baca, creating the crazy situation in which the L.A. city attorney charged the L.A. sheriff with contempt of court—*all over Paris Hilton*. In response, Sheriff Baca said, "Punishing celebrities more than the average American is not justice.... The only thing I can detect as special treatment is the amount of her sentence."

Later, Paris was brought back to court, hounded by paparazzi and helicopter cameras that covered the entire drive to court O.J.-style. The judge threw the book at her, and sent her back to jail on the spot for the full original 45 days. Hilton started crying for her mom in the courtroom. "It's not right!"

The national media had a field day with the Hilton story. The *Chicago Tribune* wrote: "CELEBRITY JUSTICE? WITH PARIS, FINALLY."

O.J. didn't do it.
Neither did Michael Jackson.
[No]r Robert Blake.
But Paris the Heiress?

Well, she's going to serve jail time.

Thank goodness.

Finally—finally!—after years of controversial legal rulings in Southern California, a Hollywood celebrity is actually going to pay for a crime.

Amazing, isn't it?

Sure, Paris Hilton wasn't charged with murder like O.J. Simpson or Robert Blake, nor was she accused of fooling around with little boys (men, maybe, but not boys) like Michael Jackson…. But, nevertheless, Hilton was sent to court for a crime (driving on a suspended license) and, unlike Simpson, Jackson and Blake, she was even found guilty of it….

Then, Sauer declared that Hilton will now serve her entire 45-day sentence, and topped it off by closing out the hearing with the statement: "The defendant is remanded to L.A. County jail. The order is final and forthwith."

As the 26-year-old party girl was led out of the courtroom to be transported back to jail, Hilton reportedly screamed out to her mother, "Mom, mom! It's not right!"

I'm sorry, Paris.

But it is.

And in Los Angeles, it's also about time. –Chicago Tribune

FOX NEWS took a more pointed direction with the story on their website: "FOX 411: PARIS HILTON BURNS WHILE OTHERS WALK."

Paris Hilton is out of jail and now the District Attorney is upset.

The whole thing has become ridiculous, hasn't it? California officials are obsessed with humiliating a blonde heiress, a girl as dangerous as a dab of Cool Whip on Jell-O….

At the same time, they don't seem to mind that O.J. Simpson, whom a civil jury found responsible for the deaths of two people, is

playing golf in Florida and laughing at them as he cleverly makes deals to collect fees for books and autographs.

Robert Blake, tried for killing his wife, is snacking in Malibu. Michael Jackson, subject of one child molestation trial and several investigations, lives in Las Vegas in the lap of luxury, travels around the world, and still entertains children at home.

Phil Spector, while awaiting trial for an alleged murder committed three years ago, has lived at home in a mansion and never spent an hour in jail. It took two whole trials to put the Menendez brothers away for killing their parents.... If they couldn't get Simpson, Jackson or Blake, and if they can't get Spector, they're going to get Paris Hilton to prove a point.

It's too funny. But that's California, and Los Angeles, specifically.

You know what guys? Leave her alone already. Pick on someone your own size. —FoxNews.com

After the dramatic hearing sent Paris back to jail, L.A. City Attorney Delgadillo issued a statement to the *TMZ* website, putting a cherry on his media victory: "This decision sends the message that no individual—no matter how wealthy or powerful—is above the law. Today, justice was served."

End of story? Not even close—this is L.A!

It turns out Rocky Delgadillo had some major skeletons of his own, including that his wife had previously committed virtually the same traffic violation as Paris—and only paid a $180 ticket as full punishment.

And this would turn out to be one of the smaller items in Delgadillo's very crowded closet. Here are some of the headlines that followed:

"PROSECUTOR'S WIFE HAD SAME OFFENSE AS PARIS"

"ROCKY'S WIFE GETS PROBATION, FINE"

"PARIS HILTON PROSECUTOR COVERS UP WIFE'S CRIMES"

"LA CITY ATTORNEY DODGES QUESTIONS ON ACCIDENT"

"IS PARIS' PROSECUTOR GUILTY OF DOUBLE STANDARD?"

"PARIS HILTON PROSECUTOR'S WIFE IGNORED WARRANT FOR NINE YEARS"

"TROUBLE AT THE PROSECUTORIAL HILTON"

"DELGADILLO NEEDS TO PROVIDE ANSWERS"

"MICHELLE DELGADILLO SPEAKS OUT ABOUT HER ARREST WARRANT"

"DELGADILLO APOLOGY, EXPLANATION NOT QUITE ACCURATE"

"DELGADILLOS ADMIT TO USING STAFFERS TO RUN ERRANDS"

"COMMISSION, STATE BAR TO INVESTIGATE DELGADILLO"

"PARIS HILTON PROSECUTOR UNDER ETHICS PROBE"

"ROCKY'S WIFE CHEATED ON TAXES"

Hey Rocky, you wanted headlines—you got them!

Not one to be left out of the media circus, Gloria Allred reportedly filed suit within days following the Paris Hilton jailhouse release, claiming her client was not released from jail for worse medical conditions than Hilton claimed.

Gotta love Gloria's consistency!

A few months after Hilton served her jail time, her TV co-star, Nicole Richie, pled guilty to driving her car against oncoming traffic on the freeway while on a combination of drugs.

She was sentenced to four days in jail, but was released after serving at total of: *82 minutes*. Hilton's other buddy, Lindsay Lohan, was not as fortunate. For her cocaine/speeding arrest she was ordered to serve a *full day*!

LAWYERS VENTING BACK AT THE MEDIA

During the middle of the Spector murder case, the presiding judge cancelled one day of trial to attend a criminal justice conference at his former law school. A full array of "celebrity defense lawyers" participated, including Tom Mesereau, Mark Geragos and Harland Braun. At some point, the discussion turned to media coverage and a debate over its impact on the jury's ultimate verdict.

It was reported in the *L.A. Times* that Loyola Law School professor Stan Goldman asked Harland Braun to explain his rationale when he went on a morning talk show and said of Blake's dead wife Bonny, "to know her was to kill her." Braun responded by joking that he was misquoted, clarifying, "What I said was 'if I was married to her, I would have killed her myself.'"

Apparently the joke got big laughs from the crowd.

When the time came for Tom Mesereau to speak, it became clear he was still upset with Nancy Grace for her coverage of the Jackson trial. Grace was well-known for never holding back her personal feelings about the pop star's guilt. She once said on air:

"Listen, I grew up standing that far from the TV screen dancing to 'Soul Train,' trying to be Michael Jackson. I won the swing championship for my age category to Michael Jackson's 'Rockin' Robin,' all right? ...If you don't have a problem with a 40-year-old man in his underwear in bed with a non-relative, [a] 7- or

8- or 9-year-old, that's your business. I have a problem with it…I've tried too many molestation cases not to care."

In classic Mesereau tone, he used the forum as an opportunity to clarify his feelings towards Nancy Grace. "There are some very professional legal analysts out there, but there are also some absolute monstrosities like Nancy Dis-Grace."

He continued, "I think her coverage of the Jackson case was sub-moronic. She didn't know the facts; she didn't know the evidence. She didn't know the witnesses. She didn't know what was happening in the courtroom…. She tried to spin a verdict through a lot of emotional innuendo that was just buffoonery as far as I am concerned. When she was humiliated by the acquittals of Michael Jackson, she lashed out at jurors. I thought she was a disgrace. I thought she was the bottom of the barrel."

Mark Geragos also spoke at the conference, and he could not resist jumping aboard the Nancy-bashing train. Geragos eloquently added that Nancy Grace was a "yapping, bleached blonde former prosecutor on Court TV."

Talking about the Peterson trial, Geragos believed Fox's Greta Van Susteren had an undue influence on his case, saying, "Our favorite expression coming in the morning before the judge was WWGS 'What would Greta say?' No matter what the ruling was the night before, whatever Greta would say that night, we'd have to revisit that ruling if she didn't agree."

During the Blake case, I personally appeared on both Greta Van Susteren and Nancy Grace's shows, and will say you are much better served being on the side of the victim with respect to Nancy. I obviously had no problem with her—in fact she would throw me media softballs on most occasions.

The thing I remember the most about Nancy was that off the air she swore like Richard Pryor in his prime—and I loved it! In fact, it completely caught me off-guard the first time it happened. Her producers had wanted me to come on their show and I had initially said no. A few hours later, I got a call on my cell phone from Nancy herself, and in a heavy southern twang, she said something like:

Eric, this is Nancy Grace. Look this fucker is guilty and I want to help you and the family tell your story. This guy is a killer, and his fucking lawyers are bashing this poor woman, and it's not right. Look Eric, I don't give a shit about Bonny's background, she is the fucking victim. This guy needs to go to prison....

Needless to say, I did her show the next day.

BRAGGING RIGHTS

To be honest, since I won the Blake case I have wanted to mention it in other trials. I don't know why other than for my ego. Trials are *so* intensely competitive between lawyers, sometimes it's just the urge to show your worth. I have never brought it up with a judge in court, but it has been tempting.

On the other hand, another well-known L.A. lawyer, Bert Fields, could not resist bragging about his famous clientele—much to the dismay of his opposing counsel. The trial involved Matthew McConaughey's movie flop *Sahara*, and Fields could not help but open his impressive trial wallet of famous clients for the jury.

It happened during the trial when a witness on the stand made an abstract reference to actor Tom Cruise, another one of Fields' superstar clients. This would be a softball he could not resist a swing at. In classic grandstanding fashion, Fields lowered his voice and asked the witness, "You know who Tom Cruise's lawyer is?"

In chambers shortly after, the opposing counsel, Alan Rader, was irate, complaining to the judge that Fields' engaged in inappropriate conduct to taint the jury. Like a kid complaining to the teacher, Rader cried foul because Fields had "announced to the jury, 'I represent Tom Cruise so I know best. I know more than this witness or any other witness.' It is outrageous, it is improper, and frankly, it was arrogant and it poisoned this trial."

Good stuff! Maybe I *do* need to start referencing the Blake case more often!

CHAPTER 10

JACKSON'S LAWYER AND
OUR JAILHOUSE BRAWL

In 2005, Barbara Walters named Thomas Mesereau one of the most fascinating people in the world after he won Michael Jackson's molestation trial in Santa Maria, California. A few years prior in 2003, Mesereau was Robert Blake's criminal lawyer when we collided head-on at Blake's jailhouse deposition.

I first met Tom Mesereau at the Burbank Courthouse before a pretrial hearing. I had been on the Blake case for about six months when Mesereau replaced Harland Braun as Blake's lead criminal attorney.

At the time Mesereau took the case over, Blake had already scheduled a jailhouse interview with Barbara Walters. Furthermore, my videotaped deposition with Blake at the L.A. County Jail was set for around the same time, and the media buzz for both was strong.

Mesereau is an extremely aggressive trial lawyer, with a degree from Harvard. He has long white hair past his shoulders, is built like a weight lifter, and wears expensive custom suits with regal purple ties. He looks more like a mad scientist than an Ivy Leaguer, but he is an absolute powerhouse of a trial lawyer.

Mesereau has the gift that all good trial lawyers have: knowing how to get to the point quickly and forcefully. He commanded the courtroom, speaking in a very powerful—yet robotic—tone, and did not waste his time in the spotlight.

Like most, I had never heard of Mesereau before he got the Blake case. Truth be told, to this day Mesereau is one of the most authoritative trial lawyers I have ever seen in a court of law. It was Mesereau's performance at the preliminary hearing that not only gained bail for Blake, but also laid all the groundwork for Blake's acquittal.

The stage for our jailhouse showdown was set a few days earlier when I met with Mesereau and Blake's other lawyers at a hearing in Burbank. One of the motions Blake filed before his deposition was to place a gag order to stop me from informing the public about his sworn testimony. You see, even before I took the deposition I had received offers from NBC's *Dateline* and *Today Show*, ABC's *Primetime* and *GMA*, and *Larry King Live*, for the "exclusive" rights to the videotape of my jailhouse questioning.

The lawyers who appeared for Blake that day were Thomas Mesereau (Blake's lead criminal lawyer), Barry Felson (Blake's long time entertainment lawyer), Terry McNiff (Felson's partner), Peter Ezzell (Blake's lead civil lawyer), and Bruce Armstrong (the lawyer Blake hired for his bodyguard Earle Caldwell).

Up to that date, Ezzell, Felson and McNiff were the biggest pains in my butt, both through the media and with their lawyering. The judge ordered us all back into the jury deliberation room to "work things out." In retrospect, I think the judge foresaw what was going to happen back there, as the tensions were running so high.

We all filed in the back room, and the five Blake attorneys postured around me like hyenas in the African desert circling an injured zebra. I needed to strike first. I had to show them all I could hold my position—even when outnumbered. Furthermore, I was still upset at some personal remarks Felson had made about me in the media, and the constant abusive letters his firm was sending.

Felson started to talk and I cut him off sharply. "Keep your mouth shut; I am in no mood for any of your bullshit."

McNiff jumped in and did not even get two words out when I turned to him. "You can also shut the fuck up; I am sick of your abusive letters—keep your mouth shut."

Like Bruce Lee, I was ready to take on the circle of attackers. I am sure the judge would not have been thrilled with the language being thrown around by both sides, but this is sometimes what happens with lawyers when nobody is watching. I absolutely had to play hardball and show no signs of intimidation.

Finally, Mesereau cleared the room of all the other Blake lawyers, and he and I sat down to talk alone. Mesereau point-blank asked me to cancel the Blake deposition, worried about the embarrassment and potential harm to his criminal case.

I agreed to postpone Blake's deposition until after the criminal trial. The only thing I asked for in return was that my client's depositions be put on hold as well. Mesereau said he could not convince the other lawyers to do that, but I stood my ground—all or nothing.

I went on to beat Blake's team of lawyers at the gag order hearing, and Mesereau held a press conference on his way out of court. He told the media that my clients and I "were trying to extort money out of Mr. Blake by taking his deposition and embarrassing him in the media, and it was not going to work."

I sarcastically responded on camera that "hearing the Blake lawyers complaining about the Bakleys using the media to taint the jury pool is like Ty Cobb accusing someone of playing dirty!"

As ordered by the court, before Blake's deposition, we flew to Memphis where Blake's lawyers spent three days deposing my clients. Blake would be next, and I made arrangements with Sheriff Baca at the L.A. County Jail for the big day.

On the morning of Blake's deposition, I arrived at the L.A. County Jail at about 7:30 a.m. The media was everywhere, lined up from across the street all the way to the jailhouse entrance. I was greeted in the parking structure by NBC *Extra*'s crew, and was hounded as if I were Britney Spears with a newly shaved head.

On the way to the jailhouse entrance, the reporters told me Mesereau had given an earlier press conference, saying the deposition was "a big publicity stunt designed for Mr. Dubin to get publicity and attention for himself at Mr. Blake's expense."

I was surprised at the comment, given that this was a court-ordered deposition that I had even agreed to put on hold. I still did not know what Blake was going to do because his other lawyer, Barry Felson, had been quoted by the Associated Press saying, "Blake would answer every proper question posed."

I cut through the swarm of media outside the jailhouse steps and walked in, heading over to where Mesereau was already waiting with the sheriffs. We then had to walk together into the jail and our conversation clearly set the tone for what was about to go down with Blake.

"What's up with the personal attacks to the media?" I asked Tom as we were walking. He never looked me in the eye, and like a prizefighter going into the ring, he said in a calm, but very aggressive tone of voice, "You said on the news that I sanctioned Blake's deposition going forward today and I never said that so now the gloves are off."

I looked at Tom and replied, "First of all, I have never in my life used the word 'sanctioned' in that context. Second, what I said was Blake's lawyers wanted to move forward with taking all of these depositions, and that is true."

We arrived at these huge, slow-moving electric gates that served as the main security wall going into lockup. We were now inside the L.A. County Jail, a vision right out of Dante's *Inferno*!

Tom and I were seated hip-to-hip on a small bench facing a Plexiglas window, with the court reporter and video camera looking over our shoulders from the hallway behind us. Inmates and guards were everywhere; we were clearly the main attraction for the day!

As I was setting up, I looked forward to see a handcuffed Blake being escorted in on the other side of the Plexiglas and seated two feet in front of us. This was the first time I saw Robert Blake in person and all I was thinking was, *"Holy Shit, it's fucking Baretta!"*

My plan was simple: no introductions, no background questions, just pull out a picture of Bonny and get Blake to confess. Mesereau had another idea. Literally before I could even get two words out, Mesereau cut me off and started verbally attacking me like Andrew Dice Clay in his prime.

"Mr. Dubin, this is a circus with the obvious intention of getting media attention...."

"Mr. Dubin, this is your fifteen minutes of fame."

"Mr. Dubin, we don't need your lectures, this is an extortion attempt on Mr. Blake...."

"Mr. Dubin, this is a charade and a clown show...."

He would not even let Blake answer his name and date of birth. Let's be clear, if the camera had not been rolling for the world to see us, Mesereau and I would have thrown down right there and then. I later found out he is a boxer, so it was a good thing the camera was rolling.

Instead, I took his verbal punches and bit my tongue. And yes, I concede, I got a few jabs in. "The only clown in here is you!" "Why do you keep referencing Andy Warhol. Is it because you have his haircut?" "What is your big claim to fame, defending Mike Tyson for rape? Nice!" [*Until then, that was his big case—now he never mentions it. Why would he? He has MJ?*]

Despite the attacks, I was able to set Blake off on a 15-minute rant some said was scripted. I beg to differ. He vented about the jail, solitary, media, unfounded rape accusations against him, and claims of putting a gun down his first wife's throat. Mesereau threatened to quit if Blake would not shut up, and Blake finally did.

This is how it went, with me asking Blake point-blank questions along the lines of: "Did you kill your wife?" "Mr. Blake, do you want to confess?" "You dumped the gun in the dumpster, didn't you?"

In turn, Mesereau answered each one by asserting the Fifth Amendment, and then rapidly firing personal attacks at me. Mesereau was completely out of control, doing everything possible to stop Blake from talking any further. Peter Ezzell was seated behind us not saying a word, knowing full well that Mesereau had crossed the line with his abusive conduct.

Finally, after an hour I got so mad that I stood up and announced a break. I then took a huge risk with my life and slid through the jail's big electric gate just as it was almost closed. The guard was really mad, but I was free to go and update the eagerly awaiting media, while Mesereau was left locked in.

I went outside and held a powerful live press conference detailing Mesereau's outrageous conduct, whetting the press' appetite for the video. When I went back in, Mesereau wasted no time ripping me apart for what he (correctly) suspected I had just done outside.

For the rest of the day, Blake sat quietly like a zombie, staring down at the table, eating an apple, and drinking a school-sized carton of milk.

After I left the jail, I was stalked by the mass media at my L.A. hotel for the deposition video. I remember Larry King offered to bump Princess Diana's bodyguard from her fatal car crash to put me on that night. I said no, and instead agreed to meet with Maria Shriver and *NBC Dateline*, and back-to-back appearances on the *Today Show*. Mesereau also appeared on the *Dateline* special with me, and I recall the ratings showing that about 13 million people watched the program.

I filed a motion against Mesereau for his unprofessional conduct at the jailhouse deposition, and requested another chance to depose Blake properly. Heated paperwork was sent back and forth.

After Judge Schacter had an opportunity to watch the entire video of Blake's jailhouse deposition, the national headlines ran the dramatic result of the fight: "MICHAEL JACKSON'S LAWYER FINED $18,950 FOR UNPROFESSIONAL CONDUCT."

And yes, he paid after losing his appeal—a total of around $22K with interest.

CHAPTER 11

SCHWARTZBACH AND
THE MEDIA

When Mesereau quit to take on the Michael Jackson case, Blake was left without a lawyer which delayed the criminal trial almost a year. Blake ended up finding a criminal lawyer from the San Francisco area by the name of Gerald Schwartzbach. Unlike Mesereau's striking superhero persona, Schwartzbach was a short, bow-tied, 60-year-old man, with a beard and curly hair he would constantly scratch.

Schwartzbach played the part well as an all-knowing scholar, complete with his tweed suits, bow ties and soft, confident voice. Unlike the hard rock, aggressive style of Mesereau, Schwartzbach was more like a jazz musician—equally talented, but in a completely different way. Schwartzbach was the kind of attorney who always found a way to win. He was not a power puncher, but would beat you down with skill, intelligence, and a charming delivery.

He and Blake appeared to have really hit it off on a legal and personal level, Blake calling him "the badger."

It is fair to say Schwartzbach and I got off to a bad start!

We met in mid-2004, when he appeared at a hearing to postpone the pending sanctions motion against Mesereau for the jailhouse fight. Schwartzbach and I met in the hall before the hearing, when Blake's civil lawyer Ezzell thoughtfully introduced us.

The fact that Ezzell was being nice *immediately* threw up red flags. It's not that Ezzell wasn't capable of being nice, but it was more likely that he was playing me for something.

I was right!

Schwartzbach immediately asked me if I would agree to continue the sanctions hearing until after the criminal trial, to avoid any potential embarrassment to Blake. Needless to say, I was not feeling his argument. However, I proposed a better idea; let's settle the whole case and I will *drop* the motion against Mesereau.

Schwartzbach tried the dangled carrot approach with me:

"Eric, my client is very interested in discussing settlement with you. However, he's unable to talk about that until you agree to remove the sanctions motion against Mesereau."

Yeah right!

Underestimating my trial skills is one thing, but treating me like an idiot? I did not see what one thing had to do with the other. Obviously the sanctions motion would have become obsolete had a real settlement been reached.

I said no, and Schwartzbach expressed the look of a disapproving father who was expecting way too much unearned respect.

We then went in to the courtroom to argue the motion and Judge Schacter was clearly impressed Schwartzbach had made the trek down from San Francisco for the hearing. Judge Schacter gave him a warm welcome, asked him to sit down and relax, and then gave him the floor.

The first thing Schwartzbach said was that as the new lawyer on the case he would *not* be holding press conferences, and would *not* be doing any TV or media. He then went into a spiel about me, and how I always talk to the media. He even accused me of tipping off the media about the hearing that day [*no comment*]. Over and over, Schwartzbach took digs at me in court for all the media coverage I had generated representing my clients.

The judge listened to his entire argument and politely rejected his request to delay the sanctions hearing against Mesereau.

Schwartzbach left the courthouse building before me—I was trailing behind after packing up my briefcase. A few minutes later, I exited the courthouse and what did I see outside? Schwartzbach giving a press conference!

Astonished, I stood on the courthouse steps close enough to let Schwartzbach feel the stare of my presence as he chatted away to the cameras and microphones. When he was done, I yelled over to him, "Did you not just tell the judge you don't talk to the media or do press conferences?"

Totally busted, the best response Schwartzbach could come up with was, "I am only doing this because you brought them here."

Once again, *yeah right!*

CHAPTER 12

PETER EZZELL AND
HIS EVIL "CRACKBERRY"

In addition to Mesereau and Schwartzbach, I had to fight against a large law firm of civil lawyers lead by the "super lawyer" Peter Ezzell. Ezzell was the managing partner of a large 100-lawyer firm in Los Angeles, and was featured in 2005 by *Super Lawyers* magazine as one of three L.A. lawyers who "can't seem to lose." The extensive article in *Super Lawyers* magazine featured Ezzell in his office holding his model airplanes. It read:

"When Ezzell isn't flying his own plane, surfing, mountain biking, skiing, or racing cars…. Of more than 150 cases he's brought to trial, Ezzell has had only three losses." –*Super Lawyers* magazine.

A few things right off the bat: Pick a *fucking* hobby and run with it! Flying, racing, surfing…. Did Ezzell not leave out space travel? Give me a break!

Ezzell was everything you would expect out of an arrogant managing partner of a big defense firm, with an inflated ego caused by dozens of young lawyers kissing his butt every day. He looked like a thin Wilford Brimley, and had the same crankiness about him. The way Ezzell carried himself and practiced law was the precise reason many people do not like lawyers—he was innately condescending.

However, Ezzell was undeniably a very skilled and dangerous lawyer, and would take you out the *second* you dropped your guard. With Ezzell, I could absolutely *never* relax; he knew every trick in the book, having probably written more than a few of them himself.

Even though Ezzell was already winning trials when I was six years old, I was *never* intimidated by him, and did not even think he had an advantage with his experience or big firm. In fact, it was quite the opposite; I felt by doing *everything* myself, and having sat through the entire criminal trial, *I* had the advantage. Maybe I was naïve, but I *always* felt I could beat Ezzell in front of a jury and never even gave it a second thought.

While Ezzell would have his numerous associates slam me with all the frivolous motions and paperwork they could come up with, he would simultaneously send me 5 to 10 e-mails a day from his little handheld Blackberry. This one is my favorite:

"Eric-

"I have had 150 verdicts and 3 losses. As far as I can tell you've tried 3 cases reported, a slip and fall, a rear-ender and your last stunning victory. For laughs yesterday we were reading your press release when you got a good lawyer relieved and you got the case. It's going to be exhibit A in the malpractice complaint Rosie files against you when this is over."

That's right, they were even threatening me with malpractice for losing the trial before it had even started. Because Rosie (Bonny and Blake's daughter) was one of my clients, I actually had Blake's lawyers looking over my shoulder to sue me if I messed up against *him*!

There was no way I was going to let *anybody* intimidate me. My immediate reply was hard and to the point:

"Don't worry about showing me your resume. That just comes with age! You have yet to impress me.... And we both know no matter how much you wish differently, you will only be remembered for beating me or not on the 'Blake' case. This case is your legacy, all the rest leading up is a wash!

"I look forward to seeing your best, you will see mine!

"No problem with a resume like yours! Right?"

Ezzell's abusive e-mails, (and my time-draining responses) went on for months. Here is a taste:

EZZELL: Professional help would assist you in your thought processes. [*He was not that wrong on this one.*]

DUBIN: How is your opening argument coming along? I look forward to hearing what you really have when all is said and done, and all your BS games finally stop. (Although you are only 1 for 25 on motions, and I was not there for your sole win.)

EZZELL: You are rapidly running out of options and there is no deux ex machina to save you. [*Never knew what that meant, and don't really care.*]

DUBIN: 12 people. You against Me, I like my chances next month! …I am just one man, you can take me with your big bad firm! Right??

EZZELL: This trial will be a minor footnote in my career but it is truly the pinnacle of yours…. As to the rest of your disingenuous comments, I will deal with those after the jury renders its verdict.

DUBIN: Go double bill some insurance companies on your little gizmo [Blackberry] and leave me alone. I have a trial to get ready for, and I do EVERYTHING myself!

EZZELL: A little inferiority complex goes a long way I see. Now that you've learned about email of course. I worry so much about you I'm out of here for Monterey.

DUBIN: Keep your digs coming, I love them! They breathe life in me and the amazing job I will do for these four children whose mother was killed by your client!

EZZELL: Your shrill cries of indignation would be truly amusing were they not so feigned. [*Yes, the guy has a good vocabulary.*]

DUBIN: This is just going to be [win] 151 for you, ask anybody who works at your firm and they will tell you you're right. [*That was a nice zinger, a little "yes men" humor.*]

EZZELL: Please do not appear at our offices on Wednesday nor schedule a reporter, you are not welcome.

DUBIN: We will see in a few days tough guy! Remember, no fighting in the court…. If you win I will shake your hand, dirty as it may be! All I can do is try my best for these kids!!!

The e-mails from Ezzell got so abundant, I actually had to ask the judge limit the amount of daily e-mails to four. Ezzell was not happy when I cut off this time-consuming tactic he had been working on me.

"This ban on emails is truly juvenile. Can u not type? Are u an intransigent Luddite? Do u want me to release my emails to jean at the L.A. Times so she can see how u comport yourself. Instead of instant communication with m…u make me fax my emails. Grow up…. U told me Wednesday that u value your professional reputation, please comport yourself like one."

A month before the trial, the tension between Peter and me was almost unbearable. During the middle of my expert's deposition, Ezzell completely lost his cool, stood up and yelled, "That's it, you and me are going a round." He then came at me from around the table to square off and fight as I sat unflinchingly slouched in my chair—feet fully extended forward.

I literally did not move an inch as he stood over me to fight.

I merely looked up at him standing over me and said to him, "Go sit down and stop embarrassing yourself, act your age." I then called the judge to see if I could get some mileage out of it, but Judge Schacter just said, "play nice, or no recess!"

In all the years of slamming me with paperwork, I only remember losing one motion Ezzell brought against me. Ezzell snuck into court behind my back (knowing I was in a five-week jury trial in Orange County) and had me sanctioned $750. I was pissed, and my e-mail to Ezzell confirmed it was full-on war:

"I heard you finally won a motion last week, nice work! It is funny how much easier it is to win when you are unopposed, but a win is a win. I can't say I am surprised you snuck into court like a little weasel, it fits your pattern of conduct.

"I have mailed your check, and made a copy for my personal file. It will remind me of what happens if I look away for even a second. I am glad to see your client reimbursed a few dollars after all your losing motions. Obviously you are ignoring his cries over poverty and milking the file for what you can with your cheap tricks.

"I am SO looking forward to finally starting trial next month. Just remember, all you have to do is beat little old me. You can even use all your firm's associates and resources against me. Your legacy should be fine, how could I possibly beat you with all your eager young associates and support staff doing your work round the clock?

"Again, I enjoy watching your fear grow with every dirty move you make! I am sure you are right, you will not be remembered SOLELY for whether you can beat me, I am sure people will also mention your Blackberry and temper.

"I will be in trial a few more weeks, I am sure you can sneak in a few more ex partes if you try! You are indeed impressive when you are unopposed! Go get em tiger!

"Happy Fourth!"

CHAPTER 13

BREAKFAST WITH "THE BOYS"
(Coffee and Threats)

After taking pot shots at me for two years about doing media, Schwartzbach basked in the glory of his criminal victory on numerous TV shows across America. Winning the Blake case clearly put him on the map, and Schwartzbach was now carrying himself like a celebrity.

I got a call from Schwartzbach a few weeks after he won the criminal verdict, wanting me to have breakfast with him and Ezzell to discuss settlement. I did not want to go! I knew that he and Ezzell were just going to tag team me with the "Blake is broke" crap they had been playing to the media since winning. I was not going to drop the case and go away, but I went to breakfast anyway.

When I arrived at this tiny 50s diner outside the Burbank Courthouse, Ezzell and Schwartzbach had already ordered and were eating. I sat across the booth from them and asked for a coffee while Ezzell mowed down his eggs and hash browns. Schwartzbach was still riding high from his criminal victory, and did all the talking. I just sat and listened to "what was in my best interest."

Schwartzbach began telling me that Blake was the kind of guy who would live in the desert and hide before he would pay a big judgment, and that my only real choice was to accept whatever settlement offer was made. Ezzell sat next to him eating his eggs in silence, while Schwartzbach continued with his sales presentation.

Finally Schwartzbach made the offer: $250K for all four kids to split. I was clearly not impressed and thanked them for the coffee. Schwartzbach then got aggressive, telling me, "You have no idea who you are fucking with, do you?"

I tried not to laugh! Was I supposed to be afraid he might strangle me with his $120 bow tie?

I just stood up, smiled, and thanked Schwartzbach again for the coffee. Breakfast had ended, but Schwartzbach and Ezzell were not done with their gamesmanship.

I next got a letter from Blake's older daughter, Delenah, demanding I drop the case and take the $250K. Schwartzbach followed up with a letter where he questioned my motives for going to trial and refusal to settle for the $250K. This was my response:

"Mr. Schwartzbach:

"I am tired of Mr. Ezzell deferring issues to you, and then you turning around and throwing them right back. Either substitute in or stop contacting me on the case. As of now you have no standing on this case, so keep your opinions to yourself. If you want to be attorney of record, bring it on!

"Your threat at breakfast 'I don't know who I am fucking with' was a joke! Be a lawyer, bluffing and taunting is not your thing. Remember, I saw you in action, I know what you bring to the table. Right now, all I see is luck and a good jury consultant.

"As for passing information to my clients, they are fully apprised of all. They are informed of your threats at breakfast about Blake living like a hermit to avoid judgment, and all your qualified statements like 'it has been represented to me that....'

"Finally, don't you dare question my motives or dedication to these four children or this case. You cried during your closing for a man we both know was behind this murder, and now you have the nerve to question my three years of dedication to this family.

"I can look myself in the mirror knowing I am on the right side of Justice, can you?

"You have done just as many press conferences as anyone, long-winded, smug and bad mouthing my client's family. You and your predecessors hit a historic low on victim bashing, and have even trashed the murder victim's children just to win your case.

"You want to see if I am the real deal? Sign up and take me on! Until then, keep your unfounded opinions to yourself. I am not interested!"

Schwartzbach dropped out for good the following week. My sole opponent would now be the "unbeatable" lawyer, Peter Ezzell, and his law firm of 100 lawyers.

CHAPTER 14

MEDIA AND LAWYERS—
USERS USING USERS

I have been a trial lawyer for fifteen years in Los Angeles, and believe me, I have gone up against some really shady lawyers. At least with lawyers there is accountability, and you can go to the judge when issues arise. However, getting upset at a TV producer for an unfair story is very similar to complaining to an electric company—useless and empty.

Remember high school? Being in a courtroom packed with an eclectic mix of mass media employees is extremely similar. There are cliques, cool kids, and geeks with brains. I have said it before; it takes a confident man to put make-up on in a public restroom at a criminal courthouse, and this was a daily event for the reporters. The sense of hierarchy is also there, networks trump cable, cable trumps local, and local TV trumps local radio.

On the print side, you have the legendary Linda Deutsch of the Associated Press. Both the judges and lawyers in high profile trials understand Deutsch's power, and give her the full respect she deserves. Linda Deutsch was chosen to be the media representative for the jury crime scene inspections in both the Blake and Spector trials, and she has covered all the big trials from Charles Manson, to O.J. Simpson, and everything since.

The AP stories are run in almost every single newspaper around the country, and are basically what you read when a publication does not send its own reporter. As an example, if you give an interview to a reporter from the *New York Times*, the article will usually only run in that paper. When you give an interview to Deutsch and the AP, the article will run in hundreds of publications around the world.

If an average day of trial lasts six hours, Deutsch has the responsibility to decide what is "newsworthy." News coverage really is that subjective, and grants the sole decision maker a tremendous amount of power!

And the truth is what is "newsworthy" does not always mean what was important, in a legal sense, to the trial itself. Lawyers are interested in entering admissible evidence for the jury to consider, and laying a foundation for a strong closing argument.

"Newsworthy" to the media is whatever makes the best headline.

THE ART OF THE SOUND BITE

The dynamic is fascinating. The news reporter wants desperately for the lawyer to say something stupid, while the lawyer wants anything but to sound stupid. It's a face-off that occurs every single time the microphones are pulled out and the cameras are turned on.

The media sets up press conferences with a preconceived plan of what they want to get out of the speaker for their story. By the same token, a lawyer should never step up to a microphone in front of the worldwide media without a purpose, strategy, and total readiness.

There seems to be an unspoken understanding when the media interviews a trial lawyer: no mercy. The consensus is everybody hates lawyers, and so the press would get an incomparable pleasure from seeing you screw up on camera—big time.

Think about when you watch the news and they show a press conference; they never show the question the person is responding to. Traps are set by very skilled reporters, and all they need is for you to fall into one for five seconds to make for a good segment.

The media's ultimate goal is to get anything that makes great news, then wake up and do it again.

There is so much about TV that is fake. The real truth lies behind the scenes in how the stories are obtained and produced. The competition in the news broadcasting business has steadily escalated over the years, with show upon show emerging out of thin air and scrambling for "exclusives" to one-up the rest.

A smart lawyer must learn how to play the media game in high profile cases, and know there are many creative options available—along with an equal number of potentially fatal mistakes. People in the hardcore journalism business are very cunning, and have premeditated angles they want to take when presenting the story.

The trick for us is to beat them at the exact same game while the camera is rolling. This is a very difficult game of cat and mouse for the unskilled camera-hungry lawyer, and it does not take much for a lawyer to look bad to an audience looking for failure.

The key to success is very simple: the less you say, the less options you give the press to change your message on a given day. For example, I would always get questions about Bonny's business and lifestyle, with the clear undertone of the questions being, "Come on, don't you think Blake had a point in killing her, she was a pretty bad person…?"

Instead of answering the specific question, I would address their unspoken connotations, and say what I wanted the listeners to know.

"I have spent years with these children, and learned everything there is to know about this mother of four and I can tell you with absolute certainty that nothing she ever did in her lifetime ever warranted her being shot in the face and killed while sitting helpless and alone in Blake's car."

Alternatively, I would bluntly state, "She did not have it coming; she did not deserve to be killed," or, "There has to be justice for her murder. She was a mother of four."

Figuring out the angle a live TV show is taking is very easy, either by simply watching the lead while waiting to go on-air or by picking up the tone of the questions by the not-so-subtle reporter. With the live shows, you can control exactly what words of yours make it on air—good or bad!

I was usually pretty strong doing the live shows, but I recall one time that I was a little too casual in my comments while live across America. It was while Blake was in jail awaiting his murder trial, and had been publicly complaining about not enjoying his time behind bars. I was on *Fox News Live* doing a segment with an anchor I had worked with many times; we always had a great connection on-air. She asked for my response to Blake's complaints about jail life, and I said, "Look, I don't wish unhappiness on anybody—*but isn't jail supposed to suck?*"

Not my finest moment, but you could actually hear the *Fox News Live* anchor laughing off camera. Because the segment was live and unedited, most viewers could recognize my attempt at sarcastic humor.

However, the opposite is true for controlling the contents of an edited TV show, where all the power lies in the editing room and is arbitrarily determined by the producers' objective. You are forced to trust that the producer will not burn you with the final product, and I certainly have a few scars!

CBS *48 HOURS* BURNS ME BAD

The genesis of a TV show appearance is a phone call from one of the show's numerous "associate producers." Their job is to become your best friend until they get what's needed for the show. If the show ends up going badly for you, the befriended young producer will be the first to agree with your frustration, but will be "powerless to help."

This leads to my horrific experience with CBS *48 Hours*.

Just before I took over the case, CBS *48 hours* aired a puff piece for Blake focusing on Bonny's background instead of the crime. Blake was in jail at the time of the story, and was clearly thrilled about the CBS story even before it aired. "Just sit back and let *48 hours* do their thing," Blake said from his jail cell.

A year later, a young female producer from CBS *48 Hours* called me, and ranted to me how unfair the previous story had been to Bonny and her family. She was adamant the family should get a chance to tell it from Bonny's side. Despite my instincts, I allowed them to interview me and Bonny's daughter, Holly, for the show.

Prior to CBS *48 Hours'* request, the only major TV interview I had previously agreed to let Holly do was with the now first lady of California, Maria Shriver, on *NBC Dateline*. I must say Maria Shriver was masterful to watch, and the toughest interviewer I have faced.

I remember first meeting her at a boutique hotel suite in Burbank, where they converted the room into a *Dateline* sound stage. I walked in, gave her a big hug, and told her I have always had a huge crush on her (very true). She ate it up, and we joked around for a few minutes. We sat down, cameras started rolling, and then she absolutely turned into a different person—a jaguar ready to pounce on its vulnerable prey.

It was because of my experience with Maria Shriver that I later allowed her to interview Holly for another *Dateline* special. It turned out to be an amazing experience for Holly. After the interview, Maria took Holly for a walk around the gardens of the Four Seasons hotel in Beverly Hills and delicately treated her like a girl whose mother had been killed. Holly needed that so much, and Maria showed the class and compassion that defines her to this day.

CBS *48 Hours* was a different story. I only had one basic condition for allowing CBS to do the segment with Holly: ask *me* anything you want, but when it comes to Bonny's 21-year-old daughter, Holly, I demanded she not be embarrassed or hurt in any way. In fact, we had extensive talks about how sensitively Holly must be handled. I was reassured repeatedly by all involved, and Holly flew to California to tape the segment. Everything seemed to have run smoothly, and we waited for the segment to air.

A few weeks later, I could not believe my eyes when I saw the massive advertising campaign CBS was doing for the show: "Special CBS *48 Hours*—Blake speaks." CBS was promoting a special edition of *48 Hours*, which would feature a whole show following Robert Blake around a Malibu house, awaiting trial.

I was never even told Blake was interviewed for our story, yet alone the sole feature. When I called our producer to see what had happened, she claimed she had no prior knowledge and that another producer did it on his own.

And then another bombshell!

During the airing of the brief segment featuring Holly and me, CBS showed a document that I had never seen before—and have never seen since—implying Holly had something to hide. At no point during filming did they even mention this to me, or even ask if it was true. It was not!

Instead, they simply concealed this mystery document during our interview, and then showed it to ten million people behind our backs.

It was my biggest nightmare come true. This young girl was the victim of CBS' lies to me. I complained for weeks, but it was in vain. The CBS producer Holly and I had trusted so unflinchingly actually cried on the phone to me, claiming how bad she felt over what happened.

Maybe she was studying to be an actress.

MEDIA AND MONEY

When it comes to the "rules" of the media game, it gets a little grey when it comes to the issue of money. To further complicate issues, many national shows are based out of New York, and the rules of ethics differ from state to state.

I would often get asked by my friends if I was getting paid for going on the various TV shows, and the answer is no. The studios would pay for transportation, and sometimes hotels if needed, but never money for the appearance itself.

The only time I was ever offered money was by Dick Clark Productions for a reality show they had called *Celebrity Boxing*. I was offered $35K to fight Howard K. Stern years prior to Anna Nicole Smith's death, when he was simply her lawyer and TV sidekick.

With some solid roadwork I think I could have taken him, but I thought best to say no. They also wanted Bonny's sister Margerry Bakley to box Lorena Bobbitt, but once again we passed. I never asked if Bobbitt would be allowed to bring her kitchen knife, but Margerry would have kicked her butt without it!

Everybody knows the tabloids pay for stories, but the mystery question is do the network "news" shows also pay money for interviews. The answer to the question is yes, they pay money, but not for "interviews." There appears to be a well-used back door that allows the media to skirt the whole "paying for interviews" controversy.

The following story, told to me by an on-air personality for a major network, explains how the TV news shows often pay big money for exclusive stories, but never label it as being for "the interview."

A few years ago, I became close with a TV reporter; "close" meaning I was great for his show segments. A few months after the

Spector shooting, he landed an "exclusive" interview with Spector's children to discuss the severe abuse they suffered from their father, Phil Spector.

After he landed the story, I asked him how he got it—and if he paid the kids for the interview. He told me his show *never* pays for interviews, although it does pay *handsomely* for family photos. Accordingly, he said, the Spector kids got $50,000, *not* for the "interview," but for permission to film a few family photos in the segment.

This common practice was recently brought to the surface in the Paris Hilton and Anna Nicole Smith cases. After Anna Nicole Smith died, the media coverage reached phenomenal heights. A few days after her death, her husband Howard K. Stern allowed CBS *Entertainment Tonight* to fly with him and film his reunion with Smith's baby girl, to whom he was claiming fatherhood.

The CBS "exclusive" ran for days, and mass speculation hit the Internet and news outlets that CBS had paid Stern one million dollars for the exclusive interview and baby reunion.

CBS denied it, and a day later a CBS producer appeared on *Larry King Live* to address the rumors and money issue. Larry King asked if CBS had paid the reported million dollars, to which the producer firmly stated, "We do not pay for interviews."

Much to his credit, King pushed farther and asked if CBS paid Stern for any photos or videos. She looked Larry King right in the eye and firmly *repeated*, "We do not pay for interviews."

She never answered the question. Or did she?

The same scandal broke during the Paris Hilton incident, the issue being whether NBC News had offered her a million dollars for her first interview after being released from jail. Hilton's parents had leaked to the media that NBC News had offered a million dollars for the exclusive on the *Today Show*.

Hilton's family indicated that NBC had offered the family a licensing fee of $750,000 to $1 million for the use of personal videos and photos, beating a $100,000 offer from ABC News. NBC quickly denied it.

The next day ABC, NBC and CBS News all said they were no longer interested in interviewing Hilton, quite obviously because of the leaked details of confidential financial compensation.

A former NBC News vice president was quoted in the media stating, "It's the way that the networks have been doing business for years. It's always bothered me, and it bothers me more now that I'm out of the business. They feel that it does not cross the line as long as they don't write a check. It's a very fuzzy line, obviously."

Another former producer came forward to discuss numerous forms of indirect compensation broadcast shows use, such as first class tickets, expensive meals and limousines, saying, "It's all built around the idea of plausible deniability so that extremely reputable journalists can say with a straight face that they didn't pay for the interview.... It's just seen as the cost of doing business. And as the competition has increased, there's been a sense of, 'What more can we do to up the ante?'"

A spokesperson for NBC News came close to admitting the practice. "NBC doesn't pay for interviews, period.... There are situations in any news story where the licensing of material is part of the booking, but I think everyone understands what is reasonable and what's not."

Obviously!

CHAPTER 15

THE ORIGIN OF A MEDIA
LEAK (The Brando Tape)

The legal strategy of utilizing media leaks has become almost as important as the opening argument—maybe more. The first dynamic in leaking information to the media is a lawyer has no rules of evidence with which to contend. In short, any information you give to the media that they are willing to air is admissible.

Now, smart lawyers pretty much understand inadmissible evidence when they see it, and that is a critical advantage these celebrities have: the media provides an outlet for lawyers to reach potential jurors with evidence that would never be admissible in court.

The origin of a jury-tainting story can be found in the jailhouse tapes of Blake discussing how best to leak an audio tape he had of Marlon Brando's son, Christian, telling Bonny that she's "lucky somebody's not out there looking to put a bullet in your head."

Bonny had been dating Christian Brando around the same time as Blake, and there was even some confusion as to whether Christian Brando could have been the father of Bonny and Blake's baby girl. The tape was deemed inadmissible in the murder trial, and there was no dispute Brando was in the state of Washington on the night Bonny was killed in Los Angeles with Blake.

However, Blake knew he had media gold with the "Brando" name, and the dramatic tape of an ex convict (Christian Brando served time for killing his sister's husband a decade earlier), warning Bonny about being shot in the head.

Blake got the tape and had his lawyers release it to CNN's *Larry King Live*, although it seems that Larry King passed it down to Connie Chung (who also had a primetime CNN show at the time). On the jailhouse tape, Blake discussed with his visitors some fascinating insights into how involved the media campaign really was in tainting his jury pool.

VISITOR: Harland was back in the news. Done 12-50 interviews. He's on Connie Chung as we speak.

BLAKE: He was unhappy with the release that Connie did.

VISITOR: They played Christian saying the phrase, "somebody's going to put a bullet in your head."

BLAKE: I think it muddies the waters for a while.

VISITOR: I'd heard a lot of those tapes; I hadn't heard that one because Harlan had given it to CNN.

BLAKE: ...I thought Marlon had the juice to keep him under wraps.

VISITOR: Marlon called Larry King and tried to get them to kill this.

BLAKE: I was much happier when Harland wasn't on television for a while, but it could have been done much better. You don't have that actor's ego that Harland has.

VISITOR: Harland's becoming a star.

BLAKE: The sister's being quiet, Marguerite? We're hearing nothing from the Bakley camp. This is good for *48 Hours*. This will double their audience next week.

Blake was again referring to the piece that CBS *48 hours* was putting together—an hour spent absolutely slamming Bonny Lee Bakley—a turning point in the case of public opinion.

After Blake's lawyers leaked the Brando tape, he assessed the damage they had caused to the prosecution's case against him. From jail, Blake vented how the *L.A. Times* pushed the Brando story back to page 3, and critiqued Harland Braun's media performance:

BLAKE: What's your take on this? The story about the tapes on page B3, the *Times* always does that.

VISITOR: Pissed off Sandi Gibbons [the longtime Los Angeles D.A. spokesperson, and the voice for the Los Angeles prosecution team on the Blake case].

BLAKE: Harland should not be bad-mouthing Christian Brando, the tapes speak for themselves. We really don't want to stick a pin in Marlon Brando, he had an affair for two years with Connie Chung, that's why she downplayed it. I think it was better when we were focused on what a good guy I am rather than what a bad guy he is.

VISITOR: I think Sandi Gibbons is right, it should be in the courtroom. I did talk to Harland, he likes being on television.

BLAKE: Did you talk to him about doing Diane Sawyer instead of Katie Couric? I got to give him a call...."

Later on the tape, Blake got even more opinionated about the fact that too many "suits" were speaking on his behalf, leading to the discussion to bring in "A-List" celebrities. During a later jailhouse phone call, Blake brought up the media strategy topic again:

CALLER: Things are breaking our way.

BLAKE: Do you think Harland's doing too much? I have a fear of Marlon Brando. I don't think we should talk about it over the phone. Quincy Jones came to see me, his best friend is Chief

Parks. He had a guy with him, the biggest guy in the recording industry. I heard Marlon called CNN to try and stop the story.

CALLER: I'm OK with Harland doing what he is doing, we're going to be doing something big, but it's got to be orchestrated. This is little stuff; it's not even the interesting stuff. It chips away at the impression that they've got a perfect case against you. Dale sent me the article from the *Enquirer.*

BLAKE: Something about Marlon gives me the willies. I told Harland to give Dale those other tapes of the other actors to listen to, they're close friends of Dale.

"Dale" ended up calling Blake after the tapes went across the country's news cycle, gloating about their success. "Harland is talking to Katie Couric, shouldn't he be talking to Diane Sawyer? The whole country's talking about the tapes."

Eager to keep their media roll going, another phone call was spent discussing the media hierarchy, and how to spread the stories to other reporters that had been favorable to Blake.

BLAKE: Couldn't you get anybody else?

CALLER: Sally Kirkland called. Shelly Winters is too old to come down.

BLAKE: Tell Barbara Walters Robert loves what you did with Delenah [an ABC *20/20* exclusive with Blake's older daughter to generate sympathy]. Can you come next Thursday instead of two weeks?

CALLER: I can't do that; she is already coming out here.

BLAKE: I'd like to give the AP lady and Larry what's-his-name stuff...we're on such a roll right now. I want Linda Deutsch because it's AP. Larry King has been a good guy. Harland gave him the tape; they took it away from him and gave it to Connie Chung. I was hoping to get her here and get her out of the way and bring the other two in.

CALLER: If I do that, Barbara won't come. The date that would work is the 15th, if I tell her the AP is coming there before her now. I was going to bring Larry King down before that but I did not want to burn her.

BLAKE: We just sit tight and wait for *48 Hours* to do its thing. Connie Chung has been sweet and gentle.

CALLER: It was offered to Larry first, but the network decided. All the people we talked to in the poll we took two days ago watch the news first....

BLAKE: Next Saturday I see Dory, Dory can find Gavin for you.

CALLER: Barbara is the most desirable market there is. Diane Sawyer is a close second. Larry King is third.

BLAKE: Deli did really well then.

CALLER: Connie is different. Geraldo is in the depths.

BLAKE: I don't like him at all.

Blake also became concerned with his lawyer Harland Braun speaking on his behalf, worried the public might feel he was hiding behind his lawyer. Blake told his friend:

"...[T]his is not my desire, this is my fucking life.... And I do not want anybody else with a suit out there.... And we'll pull that off. And this will, you know, cause we got a lot a turning around to do. Everybody in America thinks I'm guilty because I've been hiding behind my lawyer, which is what guilty people do."

Blake clearly made the decision to pull the media rug out from Harland Braun, and do his own talking. In response, Braun quit the case just prior to Barbara Walters' exclusive jailhouse interview with Blake for a big ABC News special.

Blake then went on to give jailhouse interviews to Larry King and Linda Deutsch, as well as a Los Angeles TV reporter, Paul Dandridge. It's funny, even before I got access to these jailhouse tapes I always told my wife that I felt Dandridge was in Blake's corner. He covered the story for CBS News in L.A., and every spin he took in his reports always seemed to favor Blake. Obviously, Blake felt the same.

"There's one local, there's one local news guy. I'll give you his name. He's very much on our side. Paul Dandridge. Paul Dandridge is cool."

Paul's loyalty paid off: he was the only local L.A. reporter who got an interview with Blake in jail, and he milked it for every drop.

On another tape, Blake expressed his surprise that Marlon Brando did not have enough power to stop the entire leaked tape of his son from ever airing. "Marlon had all the juice in the world, he's always kept Christian's drug antics out of everything, it's funny that he didn't do anything. Marlon is close to Sean Penn...."

With respect to Blake's ongoing media strategy, he was always focused on his primary objective: taint the jury pool and get an acquittal. Even when things did not go as planned, Blake's feelings were "it can't hurt the jury pool, that's the main thing."

Another effective way for lawyers to get a story out in the media is to include newsworthy material in a motion filed with the court. For the most part, anything filed with the court is public record and can be easily accessed by the press. It can be an effective method to indirectly plant a story.

For example, a few weeks before the jury selection began in the Phil Spector trial, the Los Angeles D.A. filed a motion to allow four women whom Spector had supposedly pointed a gun at over the last several decades to testify. The idea was to show Spector had an M.O. of pulling guns on women, very similar in fashion to how Lana Clarkson was killed in his front hallway.

Now, of course this is a legitimate motion, but the fact still remains that no matter what the judge ruled, *all* of the information was reported by the media.

As usual, Spector's lawyers cried foul against the D.A.

CHAPTER 16

CELEBRITY JUSTICE TV

The Blake case was a worldwide spectacle for many years, with coverage ranging from CNN, to the BBC, to *Access Hollywood*. It was also a front-page tabloid fixture for years, with stories ranging from true to outrageous. Even O.J. expressed an interest in becoming a TV commentator on the Blake case, but never did. (Apparently, O.J. was too busy writing his *If I Did It* masterpiece.)

Locally in Los Angeles, the Blake case was on the news almost every week, quite often the "teaser" throughout the day for the nightly news. It even got to a point where Jay Leno's nightly monologue would tie the Blake case in with local weather issues like, "It rained so hard today in L.A. that Robert Blake forgot his *spear* gun at Vitello's," or "The Santa Ana winds were howling harder today than Robert Blake at his deposition."

Leno even mentioned me by name one night during his monologue, calling me the "chief prosecutor" in the Blake case. Now I'm not quite sure what a "chief prosecutor" is, but I am certain I was not it. But hey, I'll take it—*Leno mentioned me on the* Tonight Show!

Now, I won't even pretend that I did not love every minute of the media attention that came with this case, and, honestly, I have completely lost count of how many times I have been on TV. However, the truth is, doing the whole media circuit was crucial to leveling the playing field against all the trash talking the Blake lawyers were doing to taint the prospective jury pool.

Blake's lawyers had a full year's head start before I took the case, with most people in America knowing a lot more about Bonny Lee Bakley than the murder evidence against Blake. I was always playing catch-up to show the other side of the coin, the main message being, "Bonny did not deserve to be executed, no matter what Blake's lawyers are telling you."

A good example of the media frenzy I experienced was the day I took Blake's video deposition at the L.A. jailhouse with Mesereau.

At 4 a.m., the morning after the deposition, I did the *Today Show* with Matt Lauer at NBC Studios in Burbank. I was then taken back to my hotel where I did a segment with *Extra* and numerous local news stations at 4:30 a.m. Next, at 5:00 a.m., I was picked up and taken to *Fox News Live*, where I also filmed a segment with *Inside Edition*. At 8 a.m., I was taken back to my hotel to meet with Maria Shriver for the *Dateline* interview, and was surprised to find Mesereau had been invited to join in.

Next, I was picked up and taken to Court TV for a live segment, across town to pre-tape a segment for CBS' *The Early Show*, and then back to NBC for MSNBC's *The Abrams Report*. I then rushed back to Fox Studios for *The O'Reilly Factor*, and then back to my hotel for a photo shoot with the *NY Post*. I then did local L.A. news and radio shows, and finally had some food at 9 p.m.

Another memorable day occurred during the Blake criminal preliminary hearing, when I did six TV appearances before the morning court session. Because all the news morning shows start live back East at 7 a.m., I always had to be picked up at 2:20 a.m. to be at the L.A. studios and "camera ready" by 4 a.m.

One morning, CBS' *The Early Show* actually converted the lobby of the Century City Hyatt hotel into a full-blown studio soundstage so I could pre-tape a segment at 2 a.m. before my 2:20 a.m. pickup by ABC for a *GMA* appearance.

From ABC I was picked up by Fox News, where a chauffeur drove like a madman to get me to Fox News Studio on time, and Fox even started the segment while I was still in the parking lot. I sat down in the chair literally five seconds before they introduced me to America. I then did the local L.A. news.

All of this was done before 5:30 a.m., and I still had three and a half hours to kill before court was due to start at 9:00 a.m. When I got to court, prosecutor Pat Dixon gave me a dry smile, and sarcastically joked, "Did you even sleep last night?"

No!

By the way, the sole reason all these new shows send limos for people is for the producers to have pure control. With a limo picking up the guests, the producer can dictate the exact time and circumstances of arrival, leaving nothing to chance.

Any glamour perks are completely gratuitous.

CHAPTER 17

THE MEDIA VS. A FAIR TRIAL

On many occasions, the media can use its First Amendment rights for the sole purpose of having a great front-page story, greatly tampering with the trial's progress. A perfect example can again be found in the recent Hollywood trial over the movie, *Sahara*.

In that case, the author of the book sued the movie's producers for 40 million dollars for failing to give him "sole and absolute" approval over adapting his book into a movie. The movie producers countered that the author was unreasonable in his demands, and had also lied about the book's sales figures during negotiations. The Los Angeles media followed the trial closely.

During the entire trial the judge was extremely cautious not to allow inadmissible or damaging evidence to taint the jury in any way. Accordingly, the judge held his sidebar conferences with the lawyers in his private chambers, not only away from the jury, but also the media covering the case.

The media was fuming.

The *L.A. Times* complained that the hearings were not being conducted in open court, reporting that the "highly unusual" practice of closed trial proceedings happened five times within a single hour. The *Times* also reported their frustration with the lawyers giving the media the runaround, complaining that the lawyers in the case had "offered conflicting explanations for convening in private at least 59 times during the 58-day trial."

Finally, the *Times* ran quotes from legal experts saying that only "national security interests or trade secrets" warrant taking matters into chambers for private hearings, and, "this Judge needs a little reminder of the First Amendment."

As it turns out, one of the issues the lawyers had been privately discussing with the judge in chambers was the defense's plan to introduce extreme racial statements allegedly made by the author. The judge ruled that no such racial or bigotry evidence would be allowed in the trial, and warned of a mistrial if any witness even mentioned it. "If I think it is atomic-bomb prejudicial, then I will mistry the case."

To give you an idea of how huge a deal a mistrial is, the court reporter transcripts alone for the *Sahara* trial totaled $180,000, and a mistrial would have resulted in 9,000 pages worth of trash. It would be like spending two years preparing and then building the most elaborate sand castle the world has ever seen, and then a fluke rogue wave jumping 100 feet over the beach and wiping out every last morsel.

You have to start again from scratch.

The *Sahara* trial went on for two months, and the jury never heard any of the detailed racial statements the author reportedly made towards "blacks and Jews." Then a major head-on legal crash between our justice system and the media's rights under the First Amendment occurred.

In the middle of the closing arguments, the *L.A. Times* got hold of the 9,000 pages of transcripts including the private sidebar hearings, and published portions of them on the front page for all to read.

On the cover, the *Times* ran a massive color picture of the judge and author taken during the trial with a headline that read: "HOLLYWOOD: MUCH OF 'SAHARA' TRIAL HELD BEHIND CLOSED DOORS." The story continued inside the paper, with a second headline that read: "PARTS OF 'SAHARA' TRIAL ARE BEING HELD IN SECRET."

Now, even if this jury were sequestered, which they were not, it's extremely difficult to believe a juror wouldn't have a clue about this huge front-page story. Even a juror's quick glance at the headline would create almost unreasonable temptation for anyone to read it, especially in a civil case where jurors know the end result is about money and not prison.

How could one of their spouses or friends not be tempted to share the "secrets" being kept from them during the trial, when the news had shed the light for everybody else? The jury members would be deciding the verdict and yet they were the ones being kept in the dark?

The huge article detailed many of the racial statements the author allegedly made, "I don't want any more blacks around. I hate them," and his lawyer's concern that a witness might quote the author using the "N" word.

The *L.A. Times* even quoted the judge's own personal opinions about the testimony of the 75-year-old author, who reportedly had "stumbled" through a week of testimony on the stand. "Mr. Cussler is smart like a fox, he has got an iron trap mind. He knows what's going on here."

Off the top of my head I can't think of anything more inappropriate for a jury to hear than a judge's own private opinions of the credibility of a participant's testimony on the stand. Devastating to everybody's right to a fair trial. Devastating to the process.

CHAPTER 18

LOST JUSTICE AND REAL VICTIMS

I was sitting in court with Bonny Lee Bakley's 23-year-old daughter, Holly, when the State of California shockingly lost the Blake criminal murder trial. Holly completely broke down, experiencing what I am sure Nicole Brown Simpson's and Ron Goldman's family must have also felt—devastation.

It had been a long wait for the Blake verdict during jury deliberations, and there was really no way of knowing when it would happen. With all the media waiting at court, it was very difficult for Holly to be under such constant scrutiny. In addition to Blake walking the halls, there was always a stream of cameras, reporters and producers approaching her. It was just too much.

So, Holly waited back at the hotel, while I stayed at the courthouse for any official word that the jury had reached a decision. There are only two words to describe what happens during the wait for jury verdicts: total speculation.

I made sure I was at the courthouse every morning *before* the jury, perched next to the information-craving media, watching the jurors arrive from the eighth-floor courthouse window.

What we were all looking for was whether any jurors were wearing nicer clothes than usual. Our thinking was simple: if jurors were more dressed up than usual, it was to look good on TV at the post-verdict press conference. After seeing these jurors five days a week for several months during trial, you pretty much have a feel for their wardrobes. We would also look for any lone jurors, any cliques, and whether they looked unhappy or frustrated.

Therefore, during deliberations any small variation in dress or appearance would cause a mini uproar amongst the layers of media ranks, because everyone needed something fresh to report about for that day's news. I don't think these jurors had any idea that around 30 reporters had their noses pressed to the eighth-floor window, watching their every twitch as they walked into court each morning.

Once they were back in the jury room deliberating, we would all hang out in the hallway and speculate about everything we had noticed during the 20 seconds worth of observations.

On the morning that would become the verdict day, I held my spot on the wire, looking down as the jurors walked in as usual. A few appeared to be dressed up, but we had all been wrong for several days before. At around noon I went back to the hotel 20 minutes away to check on Holly. I was walking into the hotel when my cell phone rang.

"Something is going on here, I don't know what, you better haul your ass and get back here now!"

It was my buddy, Jean from the *L.A. Times*, and she was the person I trusted the most. I hung up, grabbed Holly and got back to the courthouse in a frantic rush. Upon arrival, it was obvious there had been a *major* upgrade in security at the court, almost like a lockdown. Additionally, the media onsite had increased threefold.

Clearly we had action.

Cameras mobbed Holly and I going into court, and a complete circus atmosphere had taken over the eighth floor. As Holly and I made our way through the masses, you could almost feel the buzz outside at the media tents, and see the CNN, FOX, and Court TV camps live on-air.

Finally, the moment of truth after nearly four years since Holly's mom was killed. We were told the verdict was going to be announced in twenty minutes. As I was entering the courtroom I was told something that sent a shock of disappointment through me, making it crystal clear to me Robert Blake was going to walk free that day: "The jury had reached a unanimous verdict on the murder charge, but was hung on one count of solicitation for murder."

The D.A. was going to lose. I needed to brace Holly!

My thinking was that the strongest part of the prosecution's case was solicitation, with three people taking the stand about Blake offering money to kill Bonny. Blake even showed two of them where Bonny slept, and how he would leave her door open so she could be killed while asleep. The D.A. had hard evidence to support solicitation, including an "untraceable" calling card Blake used to plan the killing with the potential hit men.

In fact, in the back of my mind, I thought the D.A. might *only* get a conviction on this solicitation charge, without being able to prove Blake pulled the trigger himself. But clearly, if this jury did not even believe Blake asked these guys to kill Bonny, there was no chance they believed he was the murderer.

Before heading back into court to brace Holly for the feared loss, I ran into prosecutor Pat Dixon again. I told him my concern.

"Pat, if the jury does not believe that Blake even solicited Duffy Hambleton to kill Bonny there is *no way* they are going to find him guilty of shooting her himself."

Pat politely disagreed with me, saying "not necessarily," but I was convinced we were about to watch O.J. part II.

Inside court, where a nervous Blake was sitting a few rows up, I leaned over to Holly and whispered in her ear.

"Look, I want you to know that no matter what happens in a few moments it will not change how hard I will continue to fight for you guys to get justice for your mom. I have heard they are hung on solicitation, which tells me he is going to be found not guilty in a few moments. I love you guys very much, and I am telling you *I will prove this fucker did this*! Be strong, hang in there, but brace yourself for a not guilty verdict. I will handle the mob afterwards, you just stay strong and I am right here with you!"

Holly is a very intelligent young lady, and had always been very skeptical that Blake would be convicted with all his fame and fortune. I think she understood I was probably right.

We both sunk in our chairs as the verdicts were read.

Robert Blake was found not guilty.

I held Holly while she wept uncontrollably during the verdict, before quickly hiding her downstairs in the courthouse cafeteria until I could secure her escape route past the lynch mob of media outside. I then opened the courthouse front door and was bombarded on the steps by a sea of cameras.

"What is the family's reaction?"

"How is Holly?"

"Can you still win the wrongful death case against Blake à la O.J.?"

"Did you expect this?"

Across the way at the press conference, Blake and his criminal lawyer, Gerald Schwartzbach, laughed and celebrated their victory in front of the cameras. Blake bragged that he had spent "10 million dollars" to walk free. When a reporter yelled the question, "Who do you think killed your wife?" Blake screamed in anger "Shut up!" He then borrowed a knife and cut off his ankle monitor, never mentioning his murdered wife.

I was ten feet away from the microphone the whole time, holding a framed picture of Bonny for Blake to see. In a manic rush I was snatched away by a producer from NBC and flown from Los Angeles to New York for a next-morning appearance on the *Today Show*, followed by FOX News, CNN, *Nancy Grace* and then *Larry King Live*.

On one show, they played a clip of Blake laughing and celebrating his acquittal, and without thinking, I gave my honest response to his lengthy public display.

After a surreal day of Manhattan TV studios and sharing green rooms with William Shatner and Amber Fry, I checked into my hotel overlooking springtime in Central Park. I kicked back with my laptop and logged onto AOL to check my e-mails. My jaw dropped in absolute astonishment when I saw flashing on the screen: "AOL Top Story: CALIFORNIA LAWYER VOWS TO WIPE THE SMILE OFF OF BLAKE'S FACE."

Oh shit, the game was definitely on!

CHAPTER 19

THE HIGH PROFILE
JURY POOL

I am sure the Santa Barbara D.A. was thrilled when he woke up one morning to see the following headline in the papers: "2 JURORS SAY THEY REGRET JACKSON'S ACQUITTAL."

The story was about two jurors from the Michael Jackson trial, *now saying* that they regretted voting to acquit the singer of child molestation charges.

They, in fact, *believed* the singer's young accuser was sexually assaulted. "No doubt in my mind whatsoever, that boy was molested, and I also think he enjoyed to some degree being Michael Jackson's toy," the juror later said on MSNBC. "I'm speaking out now because I believe it's never too late to tell the truth."

Actually, it *is* too late!

When it came down to the important question of whether Jackson committed the crime, the jurors said, "We had our suspicions, but we couldn't judge on that because it wasn't what we were there to do. That's not to say he's an innocent man. He's just not guilty of the crimes he's been charged with."

Wonderful!

Jackson's attorney, Tom Mesereau, could not let the belated comments go, and went to the media saying,

"The bottom line is it makes no difference...it was time to move on [from the case].... Twelve people deliberated and, out of that process, justice is supposed to result. Now, two months later, these jurors are changing their tunes. They clearly like being on TV. I'm very suspicious."

THE DATELINE JUROR

Recently, Jennifer Lopez reported to the Beverly Hills Courthouse for jury duty. A few months later, Brad Pitt checked in at the Downtown L.A. Courthouse to do the same. While a sight like this might send most of America's courthouses into orbit, in L.A. it's just another day!

I have been in court at the same time as Kim Basinger, the Menendez Brothers, Alec Baldwin, and other household names. There were even several celebrities in the Blake jury pool; I remember Christina Applegate and Harry Shearer (the voice from *The Simpsons*), to name a few.

However, I must say, I was actually totally shocked when a recent headline ran in the *L.A. Times*. "DATELINE TELEVISION PRODUCER IS ON SPECTOR JURY."

Both sides on the Phil Spector murder trial had actually agreed and selected a television producer from *NBC Dateline* to be on the twelve-person jury panel. He was a 41-year-old producer, who had covered both the O.J. Simpson and Michael Jackson trials for NBC.

Even more incredibly, the selected juror had actually been working as "senior producer" on the Spector case before being called for jury duty, and had full access to many court documents during the months on the job.

And both the prosecution and defense agreed that he would be a fair and impartial juror? Wow! That may be one of the riskiest moves I have ever heard of, but I didn't really know whom it posed a bigger risk to!

In a nutshell, television producers for shows like *Dateline* do absolutely everything for the segments they work on. They are the first ones to research the story, contact witnesses for their show, and write the basic format of the segment.

My first reaction was how could this producer maintain his credibility at NBC News if he returned to work after finding Spector innocent of a crime he reportedly confessed to ("I think I just killed somebody"). How could he let Spector walk, especially now that his show, *Dateline*, had become heavily involved in working with law enforcement on their trademark "To Catch a Predator" series?

On the other hand, I totally understood the attraction to the defense lawyers. Here is a man who had access to the *mountains* of evidence accumulated against O.J., from motive to DNA, and he walked due to "reasonable doubt." The producer similarly had access to the years of court files filled with evidence against Jackson, which was also not enough under "reasonable doubt." And he was undoubtedly familiar with a "gunshot residue" covered Blake who, as we all know, was no exception to the pattern.

O.J., Jackson and Blake all had a motive, means and opportunity to commit their crimes, and yet walked free despite the evidence. Compared with those cases, Spector had very little by way of motive. The critical issue came down to whether it could have been a suicide (or "accidental suicide"), and credible experts testified in favor of both.

In fact, the defense experts Spector hired were the best and most televised experts in the world, all opining it was a suicide. This *Dateline* producer could have either viewed them as stars in their respective fields, or passed them off as well-known guns-for-hire. He was clearly a decision changer—a person other jurors could look to on hard issues. It was a risk for both sides, but a legendary move for the winner!

PICKING MY JURY FOR THE BLAKE TRIAL

Jury selection for me on the Blake case was a trial lawyer's worst fear! The overwhelming reaction from many potential jurors was that this case was "double jeopardy," or that I was just going after Blake because he was a rich celebrity. They were half right—I was going after the "rich" part. The truth is, most killers are *not* sued by the victim's family for the simple reason most of them have no money to pay the judgment.

However, I did not expect such a widely negative tone—to say the least. Did these people not see O.J.? The next morning, the *L.A. Times* opened their story about my jury selection as follows:

"If jury selection was any indication, the wrongful death case against Robert Blake could be heading for a familiar ending.... Prospective jurors rallied against the lawyer representing Bonny Lee Bakley's four children Tuesday while offering sympathy for the former *Baretta* star, who was acquitted of criminal charges in the shooting."

One exchange I had with a prospective juror that I am sure nobody in the court will ever forget was with a man I nicknamed Santa. He was a big man with a white Santa-length beard, who was extremely opinionated and long-winded. After he clearly indicated favoritism for Blake, I asked him the standard disqualification question: "If you were on my side of the table would you want a juror like you on the panel?"

This would be a question I would come to regret and his response was reported by the Associated Press around the world.

"'I have a rather highly tuned BS detector and it's been going off big time since you started the questioning,' the man said. 'If I were sitting next to you, I would not want you to be representing me.'

"Dubin appeared taken aback. 'Wow,' he said. 'Have you ever hated a lawyer as much as me?'

"'No,' the man said." —Associated Press article (8/29/05)

Another low point occurred while walking to my car after the first day of jury selection. I was discussing the beating I had just taken from prospective jurors with my "high-power jury consultant," a person I thought was going to be my rock.

"What do you think? How bad was it?" I asked her, looking for her to restore my confidence. As long as I live I will never forget her response back to me.

"Have you considered settling?"

I looked her directly in the eyes and said, "Tell me you did *not* just say that!"

"I think you need to strongly consider it," was her response.

My heart fell flat on the curb.

To make matters even worse, I was going through jury selection and into trial *without* having any of my clients in court. All of the children, except the baby, were back in Memphis. Bonny's (by this time) 24-year-old daughter, Holly, had a five-week-old baby; Bonny's 25-year-old son, Glenn, could not afford to miss three months of work without losing everything; and Jeri Lee was far too young.

So there I was alone at the counsel table during jury selection. Blake had, what I dubbed, a "Party of Five" sitting down the row from me. Blake sat at the head of the table, directly facing the jury across the long row of chairs. Next to him was Ezzell's helper, Nancy Lucus, whose main job seemed to be bringing cookies for the defense team everyday. Ezzell, Earle Caldwell and Gary Austin (Caldwell's new attorney) rounded out Blake's trial posse.

I sat alone to their right, and was closest to the jury box at the end of the long table. It felt like I was in a middle school cafeteria, as I sat alone next to the always-snickering Blake team. Not only did it suck sitting in the same row as the Party of Five, but every time Ezzell walked by the two empty client chairs to address the jury, he would place his hands on them to highlight the Bakley family's absence.

As soon as I saw the faces and responses of our jury pool, I realized that I could not win this case without Holly and Glenn in court with me everyday. This turned out to be the first and maybe most critical fight of the trial.

The truth is, the passionate argument I gave to Glenn and Holly that finally convinced them to pack up, leave the baby, and move to L.A. for three months, may have been more important than my opening.

They both came, and they were both indispensable in every way possible. It was heartbreaking for Holly to leave her baby, but then again, so was everything Robert Blake had done to this family before and after Bonny's murder.

CHAPTER 20

A TRIAL LAWYER AT THE MEDIA CIRCUS

I was a seven-year-old kid when *Baretta* was the big show on TV, and I had a few cut-off sweatshirts of my own like the tough-talking detective I loved to watch. So, on May 4, 2001, when Robert Blake's wife, Bonny Lee Bakley, was shot dead in his car, it definitely caught my attention.

I heard on the news that Blake was alone with his wife after they had finished dinner and she was shot dead in his car after he went back to the restaurant to get his gun.

Get his gun? What?

The plot thickened when it was further reported Blake had parked the car *behind a dumpster* several blocks away from the restaurant parking lot, leaving Bonny alone to get a gun he carried for *her* protection.

Blake did not drive back and run in, he did not walk back with Bonny, and not a single person saw Blake "getting his gun." Next, it was reported the murder weapon was found right next to the car in a dumpster.

It was not sounding good for Baretta!

Those were the only details about the crime itself that I can remember the media reporting on. The media angle changed drastically, and snowballed into the biggest victim-bashing campaign in modern history. The media completely switched gears, and the entire story became about Blake's dead wife's background. The source? Blake and his lawyers!

I remember thinking why is Blake's lawyer trashing his murdered wife and the mother of his baby in the media? He married her, and they had a baby together, right? Yet, the message being sent was loud and clear: *Give Blake a pass. She had it coming!*

In April 2002, following a year-long investigation that would turn out to be the biggest in LAPD history, Robert Blake was finally arrested and charged for the murder of his wife. He was charged with not only murdering his wife, but soliciting two separate individuals to kill her for money.

At the time of his arrest, I was doing a Saturday morning radio show for CBS Radio called *Legally Speaking with Eric Dubin*.

I had Howard Stern's timeslot on his station in Los Angeles every Saturday morning because Stern's show was off on the weekends. I often had guests, and took calls live on the air to give out free legal help.

One Saturday morning, Bonny Lee Bakley's younger sister, Margerry Bakley, heard my show and arranged a meeting with me about taking on the case against Blake. With Blake sitting in an L.A. jail cell a few miles away, in June 2002, I met with Margerry Bakley for the first time for breakfast at a hotel restaurant.

Margerry looked very much like Bonny, with blond hair and a pretty face. She immediately struck me as being intelligent, well-spoken and absolutely positive that Blake was the one who killed her sister.

I must admit that she was not at all what I was expecting judging from everything that had been reported about the Bakley family in the media. I myself had a preconceived notion of her, emphasizing how well the Blake lawyers were doing up to that point.

She was cool, friendly, and on a crusade to find someone to counter the Blake legal machine for the children in the wrongful death case.

With a solid combination of details and passion, Margerry began telling me the *real* story of Bonny and Blake, detailing the final months leading up to her sister's murder in Blake's car. With my jaw on the table in total disbelief, Margerry told me how:

• Before the murder, Blake kidnapped their baby, Rosie, from Bonny and gave her to his 35-year-old daughter to be raised (where she remains today).

• Bonny filed kidnapping charges against Blake with the LAPD, and Blake only married Bonny so that the charges would be dropped.

• Before the murder, Blake had large quantities of cocaine planted on Bonny in an attempt to frame and send her away to prison.

• Bonny was killed only four days after moving in with Blake in California, just a few days before Rosie was scheduled to be returned.

• Blake had often told Bonny he was going to kill her, and would even take her to scout locations for the crime.

• Bonny asked Margerry if Blake was capable of murder, and what it would feel like to get shot in the head.

I asked Margerry why all of these unbelievably important details had not been reported in the media along with Bonny's irrelevant background, and she explained that was part of the problem. I played it cool with Margerry, but this was the biggest case in America at the time and I really wanted it.

Margerry and I totally hit it off. I believe she sensed I was exactly what the kids needed—a young, hungry, fearless attorney willing to take on Blake and his lawyers every step of the way.

I would later fly to Memphis and meet with Bonny's two oldest children, Glenn and Holly, both normal kids who had not only lost their mother, but were also being vilified in the media by association. The tears in Holly's eyes would swell up when talking about her mom, bringing home the reality that this was a real family hurting terribly over her death.

The way I saw it, a mother of four children was murdered on the night of May 4, 2001, and *everything* indicated Blake had done it. I made a promise to get justice for these children for the murder of their mom, or go down trying.

I agreed to take the case. I would be representing Glenn, Holly, and Jeri Lee (7)—Bonny's children with her first husband—as well as Bonny and Blake's baby, Rosie (2). They comprised the Estate of Bonny Lee Bakley, and would share any recovery equally.

I later met with the LAPD homicide detectives, primarily Detective Ron Ito, Detective Brian Tyndall and Detective Steve Eguchi, along with the prosecutor Greg Dohi. These three detectives would turn out to be my best allies and some of the absolute finest people I have ever met. Greg Dohi would turn out to be a trusted friend, even after he left the case before the murder trial.

Getting to know these detectives and prosecutors was one of the best experiences of the Blake case, and I always felt like I had them in my corner for support. No chance I could have won this case without them! In fact, I simply presented *their* investigation to the jury.

In addition to learning the case, it was important to respond to the propaganda Blake's lawyers had been circulating about Bonny and her family. I have never candy-coated Bonny's life, and it is undeniable she did some crazy and controversial things. A big part of my job would be explaining these "things" away to our jury.

But the truth is even Blake agreed that Bonny was a very intelligent woman who truly loved her kids. She was a fun mom, who made sure the whole family sat down every night for dinner. They would have movie nights, pizza nights, and frequent family trips.

Even before meeting Blake, Bonny wanted to start a new life and move the family to California. In fact, Bonny had bought a house in the L.A. area to move her family into. Yes, she wanted to marry a movie star, but so what?

She did!

FOLLOWING THE CRIMINAL CASE

Because the LAPD took a full year to arrest Robert Blake, the family had no choice but to file the civil wrongful death case while the criminal murder case was still pending. In 2001, the time to file in California was limited to within one year of the killing, so a unique situation was created where the civil and criminal cases against Blake were going on at the same time.

After the family filed the lawsuit to protect the one-year statute, they immediately filed a motion to put the civil case on hold until the murder trial was completed. Blake and his lawyers actually fought against the family's motion to put the wrongful death case on hold, I believe, because Blake was using his homeowner's insurance coverage to subsidize his criminal defense.

Even though Blake was the one refusing to put the case on hold, the impression the Blake lawyers presented to the public was that the Bakley family was greedy and pushing the civil case forward even before the murder trial.

In any event, the criminal murder trial went first, and the scope of my trial was to be directly determined by the outcome.

Hypothetically speaking, had Blake been convicted of murder, the only issue of my trial would be how much the jury should award the children in damages for their mom's death. Furthermore, we would receive both punitive damages (punishment for killing) and attorney fees.

However, if Blake were found innocent at the murder trial, my job would be monstrous. I alone would then have to do what the State of California with its unlimited resources and best prosecutors could not: prove Robert Blake killed his wife in cold blood. Also punitive damages and attorney fees could not be recovered, the sole compensation I could seek would be for the loss of Bonny's love.

I spent several months watching every day of the murder trial, taking notes of what worked and what did not—for both sides. Watching the criminal trial as a spectator was hard. On the one hand it was virtually pressure-free being there, just having to take notes and deal with the media. On the other hand, "Put me in, coach, I'm ready to play!"

The lead prosecutor, Shellie Samuels, was a very tough and aggressive trial lawyer, who had never lost a murder case during her 25-plus-year career. I thought she was an amazing lawyer and we became friends.

Outside court, Shellie was cool, but inside she was like a force of nature. It appeared to me that Shellie was chosen for the Blake case by the D.A.'s office because she had a similar aggressive courtroom style to Mesereau. However, once Mesereau left the case and took up Jackson, Shellie wound up taking on Schwartzbach who was at the opposite end of the trial personality spectrum.

My thoughts watching the criminal trial were that Schwartzbach might win the popularity contest with the jury, but lose the case.

I was wrong. Schwartzbach won both!

MY OPENING "ARGUMENT"
(AND I THOUGHT JURY SELECTION WENT BADLY)

For me, caring or even paying attention to the media machine totally stopped when the wrongful death trial actually began. For one thing, I had no time. And even more importantly, it really hurt every time I was publicly criticized.

How could it not?

Even the numerous trial blogs from around the country would bother me, so I tuned it all out. I almost never watched the news or any of the cable shows during trial, and turned down offers to appear on them.

I wasn't nervous the night before I gave my opening argument, which was, in retrospect, a bad sign. The unknown variable going into any opening argument is how much is the judge going to let you "argue"? Contrary to popular opinion, a lawyer is not allowed to "argue" during his opening; he is only allowed to give an opening "statement" of what the evidence will show.

What does this exactly mean? Whatever the judge in that particular case says it does. Period!

Statistically, I am told, over 90 percent of jury trials are won during opening statements, and all trial lawyers agree how critical they are to winning the case. A good trial lawyer will skim the boundaries of not "arguing" their case until the judge starts granting the opposing counsel's objections.

The way I was trained by Gerry Spence, up in the mountains, was to not walk the edge of "argument" versus "statement," but rather jump off the fucking cliff and go for it. Forget the judge, forget the objections, and tell the most engaging and truthful story possible to connect with the jury.

This has gotten me into trouble in the past.

During a jury trial in Riverside, California, I was torn apart by a judge in front of the jury for being too dramatic in my opening statement. I was representing a 13-year-old boy who had broken his neck diving in the shallow end of his apartment complex swimming pool. During my opening, I was reenacting the fateful jump, *loudly clapped* my hands to simulate the boy's impact, and then dramatically stated, "Ladies and gentleman, I can't think of any sound worse than a young boy's neck breaking on the bottom of a pool."

The judge abruptly stopped the trial, called me over to sidebar, and ripped me apart for "arguing" my case too much.

Usually, when a judge holds sidebars in front of the jury, they will make sure they talk equally to both sides so the jury does not pick up on who is being scolded. This judge didn't even lower his voice, yet alone look away, as he admonished me.

The funny thing was, at the time I was *more* upset that my (supposed to be) dramatic handclap came off weak and muffled in the huge courtroom. It was so much better when I practiced it in my small office!

I remember the boy's mother being ecstatic over my performance, as we walked out of court that day! She called her sister from her cell phone, declaring me the greatest lawyer she had ever seen! She kept calling me "Billy The Kid," "Billy The Kid."

She was thrilled that I would not back down, even with the judge "all over me" in front of the jury. Not only did I win a large verdict from the jury, I believe I also won the judge over. When the trial was over the judge ordered a copy of my opening transcript, on which he had made extensive notes where he thought I had "argued" more then I needed. As a young lawyer, it was a huge compliment the judge would take the time for me.

It was literally just like the end of *My Cousin Vinny*, in which the local judge is initially skeptical of the young out-of-town lawyer, but at the clichéd end, he shakes his hand and compliments his skills.

Reverting back to the first morning of the Blake trial, I was about to give the opening of my life—or so I hoped. Even though I had convinced the kids they needed to come, there was not enough time to get them out before my opening statement, which

I knew would make it extremely hard to generate the emotions I needed.

I loaded up my car to head off to court for the big day *and my car would not start*. What a total nightmare! I was stuck at this massive apartment complex, with three boxes and a huge stack of blow-ups, and it was already 90 degrees outside. I had to call for a cab on my cell phone and 30 minutes later I was covered in sweat while loading it up, begging the driver to run the red lights so I would not be late.

My voice was already shot from the ordeal, causing my wife to break down in tears when she saw me in the courtroom. She then rushed out to get me some cough drops from down the street.

Still, I was not worried.

With the jury and worldwide media watching, I started off by introducing myself, telling the jury that I represent the four children of Bonny Lee Bakley. All of a sudden, Ezzell stood up and yelled, "Objection your honor, Mr. Dubin does not represent the four children—he is misstating the facts."

I am sure the jury had to be thinking, "This guy does not even know who his clients are?" The truth is, I did represent the four children through Bonny's Estate, and Ezzell was just trying to immediately prevent me from reaching any comfort zone or rhythm.

I don't remember exactly what I said next, but I do remember that virtually every word that left my lips Ezzell stood up and objected as "argument." But much more importantly, the judge kept ruling in his favor. Even when Ezzell lost an objection, his strategy of interrupting the flow and chopping up my opening was working.

The trick that many trial lawyers use to get around objections regarding "argument" is to begin each sentence by saying "the evidence will show." For example, in an opening you could not say, "Blake did it, he is a cold-blooded killer who wanted her dead." However, you could probably get away with saying: "The evidence will show Blake did it, and it will support the fact that he is a cold-blooded killer who wanted her dead."

Legal technicality? Yes. And it is important to get away with as much argument as possible. You don't want to sound like a rote and emotionless lawyer starting every sentence with *the evidence will show* like a programmed android.

As it turns out, Judge Schacter was an absolute stickler to the no argument rule. Accordingly, he kept on granting Ezzell's objections by the dozens, cutting me off at what felt like every single sentence. Judge Schacter would say things like, "Just discuss the evidence. Tell us what happened without the adjectives."

Without adjectives?

How could I possibly make an emotional impact on this jury without using any adjectives? I never let up, saying what I needed to say no matter how choppy Ezzell was making the water. The legal objections kept coming, but I kept on telling my story to the jury with a shot voice that was fading fast.

At the morning break, about half way into my opening, my wife ran up to me with cough drops and a Pepsi crying over my raspy voice.

I was about 45 minutes away from finishing my opening when disaster struck, with the jury and worldwide media watching. Ezzell's relentless waves of objections had finally created a perfect storm and the judge cut me off dead in my tracks.

Judge Schacter ended my opening argument before I could even talk about Bonny and the kids. My brief exchange with Judge Schacter was reported in almost every paper in the country:

"'You mean my whole opening statement is over?' Dubin asked.

"'Yes,' said the judge." (AP)

I then quickly looked at the jury and passionately interjected, "Regardless of what she did for a living, Bonny loved her kids and her kids loved her. I ask you to listen to her kids and not the lawyers."

That was all I was allowed to say about Bonny in my opening. After four years of "Bonny bashing" by the Blake lawyers to the American public, I only got in a few sentences about the real Bonny in my opening argument.

Much like the broken neck case for the young boy, I really thought I had connected with the jury—despite Ezzell's objections—and, for the most part, said everything I had come to say. In retrospect, it may have been impossible for me to generate the emotions I needed in my opening without any of Bonny's kids present in the courtroom.

Ezzell's opening was almost identical to the PowerPoint presentation Schwartzbach had used in the criminal trial, only changing the wording from "the prosecution will argue that," to "Dubin will argue that." Aside from that, Ezzell made it clear he was going to simply and methodically follow Mesereau and Schwartzbach's winning script from the murder trial—and that is exactly what I was hoping for.

That night, I called my friend at the *L.A. Times* whom I had come to know and respect and asked her how she felt about my opening. She could not mask her disappointment in me! I explained to her that it was all about connecting with the jury and telling the story.

She disagreed, and thought the constant interruptions by Ezzell overshadowed any points I was trying to make. After she was done, I asked her, "Do you think I made any good points?"

"Can I think about it and call you back?"

I was devastated, and had not yet even called my first witness.

The openings ended the week, and Monday would begin with my case-in-chief. Also, I would finally have Holly and Glenn sitting next to me at the counsel table, now making it a "Party of Eight."

I was comforted by a story Gerry Spence once told me about his experience on the Imelda Marcos trial in New York. He felt everybody hated him, and that he was being blasted in the court and press daily. At night, he would crawl in a fetal position while his client forced him to eat soup.

In the end, the jury believed in Spence and his case. He just did not know that until it was over.

A DAY IN THE LIFE AT TRIAL

To avoid a four-hour round trip commute each day, I moved into a one-bedroom apartment down the street from the Burbank Courthouse for the three-month trial. It was extremely hard to be away from my wife and two babies for so long, but I had no choice.

The apartment was more like a war zone, filled to the ceilings with Blake documents. You could not walk through the place as there were boxes and papers scattered across the entire floor. Every single night was a race against the clock to get ready for the next day.

Because a jury trial is such a fluid process, there really is no way of knowing how many witnesses you will need at court each day. It could range from one to seven, depending on you and the cross-examination by the other side. I would have to "guestimate" every single night how many people to have show up, and it is always a horrible line between wasting people's time (and maybe not even being called) and not having enough witnesses to fill the day and piss off the jury.

And when you are a one-man show like me, that means your work outside of the courtroom is just as taxing. It was a daily struggle to get the witnesses available and ready.

Bonny's two adult children, Holly and Glenn, arrived in California the weekend after the opening arguments. Holly and I had become very close over the years, and she was extremely emotional having to leave her new baby in Memphis to attend this trial.

I promised she could fly back every three weeks, and she did. I obviously felt her pain on all levels. Not only was I, too, away from my babies, my mom was also losing her ongoing battle with cancer back in Michigan.

An average day of trial would go something like this. I would get up at about 5:00 a.m. to finalize witness questions, prepare exhibits, pick up Bonny's kids and then head to court. Court would be in session from 9:00 a.m. to 12:00 p.m. My amazing wife, Dalia, would take care of our kids each morning in Orange County, and then drive several hours each way to be able to watch me in court. While Holly and Glenn had lunch with Dalia, I would spend the entire lunch break frantically preparing for the afternoon session, researching any surprises that had transpired in the morning session.

I would then head back to court, cut through the media, and the afternoon session would go from 1:30 to 4:30 p.m. From 4:30 to 5:00 p.m., the lawyers would meet with the judge to finalize the witness list for the next day, and go through any legal issues and problems.

On the drive back to the apartment, the kids and I would re-hash the day in detail, most days pleased with the day's testimony. Sure, there were some bad days, but the truth is in trial every single day is a separate battle, and I felt pretty good that I was winning a majority of them.

However, just like a boxing match, you never know what is on the judge's scorecard until it is over and too late to change anything.

We would get back to the apartment at around 5:30 p.m. and that is when I would have to work the hardest, all through the night. I would usually spend 5:30 to 10:00 p.m. calling the witnesses I would need for the next day, setting up a time for them to appear at the courthouse.

Sometimes I would have to go at night to meet a witness for coffee (or even drinks), just to ease their mind face to face. Other times, I would have to beg for them to appear at the trial. I did have the power to subpoena people, but that meant bringing them in angry, which is not an ideal way to finesse what you need from critical witnesses.

I had about 50 witnesses I needed to show up, ranging from the very busy homicide detectives to the men Blake had solicited to kill Bonny. The fact that most of these witnesses had already appeared at the criminal trial, and had been subjected to attorney and media ridicule in a losing effort, did not help my job at all.

After securing and preparing the witnesses I would need for the following day, I would usually order a pizza from the same exact place every night. This was not superstitious—they just had really good pizza.

From 10 p.m. until about 3:00 a.m. I would work on legal issues for the judge, organize documents, and continue prepping for Blake's upcoming testimony and my closing argument. I would try and sleep from 3:30 until 5:00 a.m., usually with the lights still

on under mounds of transcripts and documents covering
my bed.

When 5:00 a.m. came each day, I would repeat the frantic
22-hour-day process. This lasted three months.

I can't even remember how many nights I panicked that not
a single witness would show up at court the following day. I used
the two kids as my witness insurance cards, warning them each
morning I would have to call them to the stand that day if
somebody failed to show up. Through a combination of obsessively
hard work and flat out luck, I never missed a beat with my witnesses.

The best part about this grueling trial process for me was
the six hours each day I actually stood before our jury presenting
my case. When you shine in court, it not only makes the self-
imposed torture of the previous 24 hours amazingly worthwhile, it
also reminds you of how important the next will be. It is like a
double shot of espresso pumping you with energy and adrenaline,
when in reality you are both physically and mentally drained.

What is even better is that when you are in action during
trial, you are forced to stay solely focused in the moment, and not
worry or even think about anything else. It is during the 18 hours
each day you are not inside court that you freak about every single
detail, not only about the trial, but all the other things in your life.

There have been several occasions where my body has
completely broken down immediately following a trial—once the
mask of adrenaline, competition, and mandatory 100% effort was
lifted. More than once, I have wound up in the hospital after
completing a trial, and those were only trials that lasted a
few weeks.

THROWING EZZELL A CURVE BALL

One critical thing I learned from watching Ezzell's well-polished PowerPoint opening argument was that he was going to follow Schwartzbach's script from the criminal trial to the T. I had anticipated this, and specifically crafted my case to avoid all the witnesses and issues that I observed worked to Blake's advantage during the murder trial.

I felt I had a huge advantage over Ezzell because he had not been at the criminal trial. I did not miss a day. If I could not avoid a negative witness or piece of evidence, I would at least diffuse any bombshells to minimize their impact before Ezzell could stand up and launch.

Right off the bat, I started with a curve ball, focusing on the evidence against Blake's handyman/bodyguard, Earle Caldwell, who had been dropped from the murder case before the trial. I knew Ezzell had very little on Caldwell in his cloned "trial in a box" script because he was not a defendant in the murder trial.

Many of my opening witnesses had not been used in the murder trial, including Caldwell's former fiancée who identified that the murder weapon belonged to Caldwell. I also called an LAPD computer detective, who verified Caldwell had been researching homemade silencers on the Internet a few months prior to the murder.

The media was reporting this as "new evidence."

When I put Caldwell on the stand, one of my first questions to him was whether he had driven to Arkansas at Blake's request, in an attempt to plant cocaine on Bonny and have her falsely sent to prison. Initially, he took the Fifth Amendment, which drew a large gasp from the jury. The judge then ruled he could not take the

Fifth Amendment on this issue and Caldwell then made an angry remark about the LAPD being a bunch of liars.

Finally, Caldwell admitted driving a package out to Arkansas at Blake's request, but claimed he did not know what was in it. I also got Caldwell to admit he was hiding in Blake's house the day Blake reportedly stole the baby from Bonny, admitting he was there in case things got "ugly."

I also called to the stand a person Caldwell had been close friends with for many years, who had also not been used in the criminal case. She testified that shortly before the murder, Caldwell asked her to help him get an unregistered gun, and a few days after that, he left her a suspicious voicemail about leaving town—possibly to establish an alibi. After the murder, she said that Caldwell made a disgusting comment about Bonny deserving to die.

Finally, I hit the "murder list" found in Caldwell's car, containing items such as "two shovels," "25 auto," and "old rug." I asked Caldwell about a trip to the desert he had taken with Blake a few months before the murder. Caldwell had denied this trip to the police, and neither he nor Blake could recall where they had slept during their two-day excursion.

Caldwell went with Bonny and Blake on a "honeymoon" trip to the desert a few weeks later. During the trip, he drove Bonny's car back to California and searched through Bonny's personal belongings, at Blake's request, to "see what she was up to."

As a major bonus, I also got Caldwell to say some extremely nice things about Bonny as a person, including her taking Caldwell to the ER during the honeymoon trip and staying with him until 3:00 a.m. to make sure he was well before taking him back to the lodge. He also talked about the time Bonny gave him gambling money and refused payback even after he ended up winning.

It was the same for every witness. I knew where Ezzell was specifically going with each cross-examination, while doing my best to keep him guessing and confused by the major modifications I was making.

For example, when I had the LAPD homicide detective on the stand—the man who did the gunshot residue test on Blake—I knew Ezzell had a big posterboard blow-up from the criminal trial which identified the GSR testing procedures the LAPD had violated. Ezzell was licking his chops to nail the detective with it, but I never gave him the chance.

In front of the jury, I walked over to Ezzell's big pile of blow-ups, and pulled that particular one out. I showed it to the detective and did my best to diffuse every grenade Ezzell was set to throw at him. In fact, Ezzell was so pissed off he stood up and complained to the judge, in front of the jury, that *he* should be the one to use his blow-ups first.

I loved it!

I stole his thunder at every opportunity, and knew *his* case better than he did! I had watched both Mesereau and Schwartzbach use the same exact blow-ups and arguments at trial, and knew Ezzell's strategy would be a carbon copy.

It was like having the answers to a test, or at least knowing what the questions would be.

BRANDO, CRACK MONKEYS AND OTHER TRIAL SURPRISES

Most trials have a surprise left hook, much like the toy at the bottom of a Cracker Jacks box. You know it's there, but you don't know what it is until you get to it.

A recent example that comes to mind is a wrongful death jury trial I did for a 23-year-old kid suing for the lost love and financial support of his stepfather after a fatal motorcycle crash. His mother had a different lawyer, a lawyer who had advised my client he had no case, and only agreed to take on his mother. I took his case.

The mom's lawyer settled for virtually nothing. I rejected the lowball offers to settle, and went to trial. I was doing great, until the defense called a surprise witness, *my client's mom!* She testified *for the defense* that my client never got along with the step-dad, never got any financial support from him, and was in fact kicked out of the house at 17. It could not have been worse, as her attorney sat in the courtroom with a smug smile on her face.

Believe it or not, I still won a huge jury verdict.

In the Blake trial, Christian Brando was my Cracker Jacks toy. After being thrown out as a suspect in the criminal trial, the judge let in all the Brando evidence at ours. Brando turned out to be the main focus of the Blake defense. Christian Brando had killed before, and Ezzell was allowed to repeatedly play the audiotape of Brando yelling at Bonny, "You're lucky somebody ain't out to put a bullet in your head."

The truth is I *never* believed Ezzell would be able to serve a trial subpoena on Brando since he lived outside the scope, in Washington. I even bet Ezzell dinner on it.

Wrong!

Brando showed up late on a Wednesday morning with only two weeks left in the trial. While waiting for him to arrive, I found his lawyer in the hallway, and I asked him what Brando was going to say on the stand. He told me "he will not be answering any questions, and I will be instructing him to take the Fifth on everything. I know it sucks for your case, but that is what we are going to do."

Fucking great!

I begged him, "Why take the Fifth and make that the headline across the nation: 'BRANDO TAKES FIFTH TO KILLING BLAKE'S WIFE'? Why not just tell the truth and get on with his life? I'm winning!"

He just said no, they did not want to open any can of worms so would take the Fifth on everything to play it safe. Just then Brando came walking in, while the media outside went crazy. I went upstairs to get ready for trouble.

Brando took the Fifth Amendment over 30 times, even when asked the crucial question of whether *he* killed Bonny. This would have been bad enough, but Brando did something on the way out that could have resulted in a fatal mistrial.

Out of nowhere, while Brando was leaving the witness stand, he walked past the jury box, pointed at Blake and mouthed to the jury, "The asshole did it."

A few jurors laughed when he walked out, but I think the judge and Ezzell missed it because Brando had covered his gesture with his coat jacket and obstructed our views. Court TV reported it that night, and so did a few of the jurors in the morning. I knew there would be trouble, and I was right.

The trial was put on hold, and we brought in each juror (all 16) individually into chambers to question them on what they saw and how it would affect them. Responses varied from, "I thought Brando was a fucking asshole" to "where is he getting his information?" "what a jerk," "he was high on something," and "he pointed at Robert."

Robert? When did my jury get on a first name basis with the defendant I was trying to prove was a cold-blooded killer?

Brando was elevated to the top of the jerk tree, even more than Blake. He was now receiving way too much attention just as the defense was about to start calling witnesses to support the Brando theory.

The judge set a "contempt of court" hearing against Brando, who would be facing jail time for his conduct. I lost a lot of momentum with Brando, and now a string of witnesses would claim his involvement in the crime.

On another day, Ezzell called to the stand the same "drugs expert" from the murder trial, to discredit the two men Blake solicited to kill Bonny. He was just going to say that, in general, people who do drugs can be delusional so these guys should not be believed.

I was holding my breath during the whole direct examination by Ezzell, hoping he would not bring up the crack-smoking monkeys incident.

That's right, the crack-smoking monkeys incident!

It was an outrageous moment at the criminal trial. This same "drugs expert" volunteered on the stand during the murder trial that he smoked crack inside cages in the basement of UCLA with caged monkeys. In fact, I had an article framed about it in my office: "CRACK-SMOKING MONKEYS ENTER BLAKE TRIAL."

During Ezzell's long and boring direct-examination, I prayed he would miss this revelation, so I could get a big laugh while showing the jury this expert was *loco*. Two hours later, Ezzell was done, *and he missed it!* I wasted no time, and with a deadpan delivery, said,

"Sir, I apologize in advance for the drama, but I have been waiting my whole career to ask this question: Isn't it true that you smoked crack with monkeys?"

The jury looked at me as if I were totally crazy, and Judge Schacter cut in even before the witness could answer, "You do not mean actually crawling in monkey cages with a crack pipe, do you?"

"Yes I do, your honor!"

All of the jurors' eyes then turned in unison to the expert witness for his answer: "Yes, but that was back in the 1970s."

The Blake wrongful death trial contained many crazy moments leading up to Robert Blake taking the stand, including a witness that suddenly had to catch a plane out of the country after meeting with Blake's private investigator in the hallway. (Judge Schacter made him stay.)

On one occasion, Caldwell's lawyer fell asleep while Ezzell boringly questioned his expert on gunshot residue. He leaned back so far in his chair, it began to fall, and I caught it and saved him from a backwards summersault onto the courtroom floor. (He smiled and thanked me.)

On another day, the judge made me call an ex–New Jersey mafia hit man from court on Ezzell's speakerphone (outside the jury's presence), to confirm my diligence in bringing him in to testify. This was typical Judge Schacter—I think he just wanted a chance to have a *Sopranos* moment, and have some fun questioning a "wise guy" in open court.

He actually picked up, verified I had been calling, and said he had lost too much street credibility by testifying at the murder trial to do it again.

There was also true courtroom suspense—a Perry Mason moment that could have cost me the whole trial. I made a game-time decision to ask Earle Caldwell's girlfriend a question nobody had ever asked her before: Did she believe that Caldwell and Blake were responsible for Bonny's murder? She was a witness who was spending time with Caldwell and Blake leading up to the day of the murder; a woman Caldwell had loved and clearly confided in. In fact, after the murder, Caldwell had asked her to clear things out of his apartment before the police could obtain a search warrant, and she had.

Aside from breaking the cardinal rule of never asking a question you do not know the answer to, this was potentially a deal breaker if she said no.

Dead silence filled the court as I asked, "Based on everything you saw, and putting aside who actually pulled the trigger, do you believe that Robert Blake and Earle Caldwell were involved in the killing of Bonny Lee Bakley?"

Tears filled her eyes as she paused for what seemed like a decade, and then she leaned into the microphone and said that yes, she did believe they were involved.

Even though I felt like I was pitching a great game, I knew whatever happened with Blake on the stand would change everything one way or another. It needed to be the performance of his lifetime, and I felt the same about what I had to do. If he was going to beat me, he was going to have to beat my best!

I would spend all my extra time at night during the trial, and virtually every waking hour of the weekends preparing to put Blake on the stand. In fact, I kept pushing the date back just to give me more time to keep preparing.

But then something happened that told me the time was right. It was now time to square off with Robert Blake—*and man was I ready!*

SHOWDOWN WITH BLAKE
(GOOD THING FOR METAL DETECTORS)

"Jurors gasped, the judge made awkward jokes, and Robert Blake apologized after barking orders at court personnel during his first day on the stand Thursday at his Wrongful Death trial. And that was just the first 15 minutes." –Courttv.com

Tensions were running high the day before I decided to put Robert Blake on the stand. During the morning break, I was standing at the counsel table and happened to look over to my left to see Blake staring me down. I was in no mood for his bullshit, and sharply snapped at him, "*If you've got something to say to me, then go ahead and say it!*"

Blake completely lost control and started to charge at me for a fight! With his fists in the air, Blake was punching through his lawyers trying to get at me while screaming, "*I know how to talk!! I know how to talk!*" Blake was finally subdued by his attorneys before he could get at me, and the jury never saw what happened.

During the entire ruckus, I never broke eye contact with Blake, and never moved an inch as he lunged to get at me. Right there and then I made the decision to put Blake on the stand as my next witness. The time was right to push his buttons.

The next morning, before a packed courthouse, I called Robert Blake to the stand. It would turn out to be a historic seven-day courtroom battle, a legal fistfight that predictably turned out to be for all the marbles.

My plan was simple: no fluff, no warm-up questions, come at Blake Mike Tyson style at the opening bell! It turned out he had the same idea, and together we did not disappoint those expecting high drama.

"Good morning Mr. Blake. How many times would you estimate you have lied under oath since your wife was killed in May 2001?"

Blake was not happy.

"I couldn't make any estimate because I haven't lied under oath."

I then pulled out a stack of documents and told Blake I'd start by addressing his first lie.

Blake quickly lost his charm and composure; I had him furious and venting within 30 seconds. During another exchange, Blake dramatically testified that the cops had been pointing the finger at him from day one and he screamed at me,

"How would you feel if the cops accused you of killing your wife?"

Without the slightest hesitation, I snapped back, "Well, did you kill your wife?"

"I beg your pardon, sir?" Blake stumbled.

"Did you kill your wife?" I firmly repeated.

"No," Blake said, warning me, "don't get cute."

I *never* let up.

"Would you say your handyman, [Earle] Caldwell, had a hobby of murder?"

"No," Blake shouted, "and whoever said that, I will say they are rotten, foul liars to the core."

"Are you having fun?" I snapped back at Blake as I approached Holly and Glenn and reminded him in front of the jury that their mom had been killed.

"I beg your pardon?" Blake said sternly.

"What's the next question?" the judge cut in.

"He just asked me if I'm having fun. I want him admonished!" Blake said.

"Stop, stop," the judge said.

But Blake could not stop.

"I want to answer the 'Am I having any fun' question," he said.

"Remember what I told you," the judge said. "Calm down. Next question."

The judge was referring to a picture he had actually drawn for Blake after our first round of fights. He handed Blake a piece of paper in front of the jury with a big pink circle drawn in the center. "Don't let him push your buttons," Judge Schacter told him. "Use the picture as a reminder."

Blake could not follow the sound advice.

I next asked Blake a rhetorical question and he went off on a maniacal rant:

"He's lying! He's lying!" Blake told the judge.

"That's just lawyer talk," the judge joked back.

"He's lying. He gets to do that?" Blake said. "I thought only cops could do that."

Blake was coming off badly, not showing the charm I had feared he would! He kept avoiding answering my hard questions with one-liners like. "You have an elaborate imagination, sir." or "Counselor, get yourself together." Over seven days he would call me "Junior," "Sonny," and "Chief." When I would catch Blake changing his story, he'd say in his classic *Baretta* voice: "There's a whole gang of stuff that I never said to you, boss, a whole gang of stuff."

Early on, I implied to the court that Blake wanted special treatment during his testimony and he once again freaked out. Totally miffed by my accusation, Blake began to motion to the court reporter as if she were his personal assistant and began barking for her to read back any testimony in which he asked for any special treatment. Obviously the poor court reporter ignored his repeated requests and kept typing until Judge Schacter finally cut in and joked, "All right. So, you don't want any special treatment!"

Not more then 20 minutes later, Blake requested and was granted a private meeting with his lawyer in the witness box, in the middle of my questioning—no special treatment indeed!

I kept Blake on the stand for seven days, and asked him everything possible! If Blake would not respond as I needed, I would pull out his deposition transcript and read from his previous sworn testimony. He had swayed so much on important issues, I had him impeached no matter what he said!

There was evidence Blake was showing nude pictures of Bonny (from her 20s) to potential hit men, in order to show that the murder was necessary to protect their baby from exposure to her. When questioning Blake on such a meeting, he admitted he did show one of the solicited "hit men" the nude photos.

I said, "So not having seen Duffy in 20 years, the first thing you did was pull out nude photos of your wife?"

The court clerk literally fell out off his chair, and they both crashed loudly to the floor, causing an uproar in the courtroom.

When Blake complained that Bonny had tricked him and lied about taking birth control pills to get pregnant, I walked up to the witness stand and handed Blake a red box of Trojan condoms and asked, "Can you please tell the jury whether you know what these are."

Blake replied, in a low Italian accent: "Condoms and I never got along very well."

In order to expose Blake's attempt to con Bonny into an abortion, I later asked Blake, "You faked getting cancer, didn't you?" At first, Blake denied it. Then I played a tape of a secretly recorded phone conversation of Blake trying to convince Bonny to have an abortion, on which he says: "I have colon and prostate cancer, they're trying to shrink it...the treatments are a mother fucker."

Blake then changed his answer to, "I could easily have said that."

I next made the humorous mistake of asking one too many questions on the topic.

"Did you also tell Bonny Lee Bakley that you had Alzheimer's?"

"I don't know," Blake responded.

"That's an interesting answer!" Judge Schacter deadpanned with perfect timing, getting a huge laugh from the courtroom.

Then it flat out got ugly. After seven long days of being drilled by my questions (I am sure he had never been spoken to like that since puberty), Blake said something that Court TV dubbed their quote of the week, even beating Sadam Hussein (while he was still alive).

Blake barked out at me from the witness stand, "Don't get cute with me, chief, or we're going to start talking about your personal life. I know a lot about you, and what I don't know I can lie about."

"Is that a threat?" I asked.

"It's not a threat, it's a promise!" vowed Blake.

When I had cornered Blake about his inconsistent testimony to the police regarding his claim to have left his gun at the restaurant, telling separate versions of leaving the gun "on the booth" and "under the booth seat on the floor," he again became very angry and evasive. He started complaining about how the police were treating him like a suspect, stating,

"I have a vague recollection of that mess, I was doing the best I could. If I said 'under' instead of 'on'—*shoot me.*"

"No, thank you," I responded, without missing a beat in my timing.

Blake told the jury he dated Bonny because "I didn't have much of a life. I was very, very single—very much a loner. And there aren't many women who will simply just sleep with you and get back on the bus, if you know what I mean. With Bonny, pathetically, a part of me required that—that 'help me make it through the night and I'll see you later.'"

After four years of relentless victim bashing by his lawyers, Blake proved positive in confirming that Bonny loved her children and had much to offer.

"Bonny liked to talk…. She was extremely intelligent. I would guess her IQ at 150. She could charm the eyes out of a rattlesnake."

Blake also tried to indirectly point the finger at Marlon Brando as being behind Bonny's murder, claiming Marlon was extremely disappointed when Bonny's baby (originally named Christian Shannon Brando) was ultimately confirmed to be Blake's. He had stated Marlon was devastated to lose this grandchild he thought Bonny had given him and that he was afraid of Marlon Brando and his power, saying, "He [Marlon Brando] was angry."

On Blake's final day on the stand, he asked the judge for permission to ask *himself* a question, and Judge Schacter said *yes!* Blake then asked himself in a mock lawyer voice, something along the lines of, "Mr. Blake, last week you said you knew things about Mr. Dubin, and he asked you if that was a threat, and you said it was a promise. What did you mean by that?"

I was thinking, *You have got to be kidding me!* The judge was now going to let Blake charm his way out of seven days of damaging testimony? To at least make his performance more difficult, I jumped in and cut Blake off before he could answer his own question.

"Actually Mr. Blake, if you want to be accurate what you said was what you could not find out about me you would lie about."

Blake acknowledged this omission to the jury, and re-asked the question to himself incorporating my input. Blake then said to me, right in front of the jury:

"When this is over, some people should know I am no longer going to sit on the sidelines. If some people don't learn to behave themselves, I will enter their lives and teach them some manners. I will find them and become their personal Bubba and no longer hold back. I will even go to their wives...."

I could listen no more. With the riveted jury watching, I stood up, cut Blake off mid sentence and yelled at him, "*You better bring your gun again!*"

After the final day of drilling Blake on the stand, I must admit, I was afraid for my safety. I felt like maybe I was not taking Blake's threats as seriously as I should—the same fatal mistake Bonny had made.

Later that night, I went back to my apartment for the nightly routine of ordering a pizza and working all night until I passed out. When I opened the door for what I thought was my food, instead standing over me in my door was a man wearing a white *Scream* horror-movie mask with a black hood draped over his head.

For a very long split second I thought, *I'm dead.*

I then glanced down and saw the pizza box in his hands and remembered it was October 31st: Halloween.

CLOSING "ARGUMENT"

At the time I was writing my closing argument, I did not think it was the "do or die" to winning the trial. It turned out, it was! I was later told by the jury that, for many, my closing was what finally put all the pieces together in proving Blake killed his wife.

I had gotten such mixed reviews over my opening, I really just wanted to nail the closing argument to show what I could do! I knew the three lead homicide detectives were coming to watch and show support, and that was on my mind as much as the jury. This closing would culminate four years of unbelievably hard work by all involved, and this was the last chance for any justice.

I had never used a computer PowerPoint presentation before, but the more I played, the more I liked what it could do. It was like a high-tech slide show; I could create each slide and control the mood and tempo through colors, words, and photographs. For example, my slide presentation began with a blue background and yellow writing, but abruptly switched to black with red writing when I transitioned to the night of the murder, and to lavender and pink when I talked about Bonny and her love for the kids.

I worked like crazy to put together this closing during the two-month trial, mostly in the middle of the night after I had finished preparing for the next day's witnesses. Every weekend I would spend 18 hours a day on the closing—I was obsessed with perfection.

300 hours later, I knew it was powerful.

Far and away, my biggest fear was that my computer would not function or some technical problem would screw me. I arrived early for that reason alone, to make sure my laptop PowerPoint presentation worked with the court's projector, just like it had in the test run a few days earlier.

It did not work.

I tried everything. It would still not work! Everyone in the packed courtroom was waiting for me to start, and I was in a cold sweat panic. Every minute seemed like an hour, and nothing would make the projector work.

Now, I cannot prove that Ezzell pushed a few mystery buttons on the projector to sabotage my closing, but at the same time, I had *no doubt* about it. He had been using his PowerPoint for two and half months on that projector, and he at least knew *exactly* why it would not work. When I asked him for some help, he refused and said, "I guess you're going to have to do without it."

My ass!

I asked Ezzell if we could plug in his laptop and see if it was a projector problem or my computer. He refused, and turned away to ignore me—total confirmation he was the cause of the "technical problem."

I told the bailiff what was happening, and she managed to find a county computer technician who came into the court, pushed two buttons, and made it work!

The judge then let the jury in. It was showtime!

For pure sportsmanship, before I began I walked over to Ezzell and leaned down whispering in his ear, "You are a great lawyer!" Obviously caught off guard, he responded with a sincere, "Thank you very much."

I then went on to deliver the best closing of my life. I simply nailed it! After I finished, I remember walking over to a very bright reporter with the *L.A. Times* and asked him if he thought I did OK. With his massive vocabulary locked and loaded, he could only respond, "Yeaaah…yeaaaahhhh!"

I had him speechless!

The detectives were equally blown away, a victory in itself. My wife saw me at my best, and that also meant the world to me. No question about it, I felt confident I had proved Robert Blake killed his wife!

I intentionally did not put a dollar amount in my closing. I simply told the jury they had earned the right to make that call if they found Blake liable. My thinking was I could only underbid myself, and if I won, they might come back with an amount *way* higher than I was thinking. (Ezzell would later make the biggest mistake of his career, arguing Bonny's life was worth "$0.")

Before Ezzell started his PowerPoint presentation, he came over to me and shockingly complimented my closing: "Looks like we finally found something that you are good at." It was the only nice thing he had ever said to me before that moment, and certainly since.

He would then talk for about four hours, starting off strong, but running out of steam half way through. I remember thinking, "How many hit men can this guy possibly explain away?" It just seemed like he was climbing too high a mountain. I had stacked up far too much evidence for him to lawyer his way through.

Towards the end, Ezzell was clearly losing his voice. Without even looking at him, I reached back over my shoulder and handed him a box of cherry cough drops in front of the jury. Ezzell took one, handed back the box, and finished his closing.

The point I had made was strong and simple: I wanted the jury to clearly hear everything Ezzell had to say—he was *not* hurting my case.

After Ezzell finished his closing, I had the final chance to speak to the jury to close the trial. Any passion my closing may have lacked because of the PowerPoint presentation, my rebuttal argument made up for tenfold. In fact, I feel my rebuttal may have even been stronger than my closing. There was no script and no slide show—just me, and raw emotion responding to everything Ezzell had argued.

I held back nothing.

I hammered Ezzell for the $0 argument about Bonny's worth as a mother. I took a marker and proceeded to draw a huge

"0" on the board, writing the word "LOVE" in the middle. I told the jury,

"Nobody is a zero, *nobody*. A mother who loves her kids is priceless, and there is no dispute Bonny loved these kids and these kids loved Bonny."

At the very end, I walked over to the jury and told them that after four years my job was done. I had kept my promise to these four children, and had given my heart and soul to get justice for their mom. With tears in my eyes, I told them it was now time to turn over the responsibility to them! I begged them to take their time, and look at all the evidence against Blake.

"There has to be justice," I passionately pleaded. "He killed their mom, there has to be justice!"

CHAPTER 21

THE VERDICT

I knew a quick verdict would mean I had lost.

There were two big questions that would take some time: Did Blake do it? And, if the answer was yes, was she a good mom? The second question was a major hurdle that many people thought I could not clear, and if I did, it would only be for a small amount.

After the first few days of waiting, I became numb. My body was beginning to shut down and I was too mentally and physically spent to dwell on anything. Holly and Glenn could not wait any longer to return to Memphis, so I waited alone for the jury to return their verdict.

One of the things that gave me hope during the wait were some of the questions the jurors were allowed to submit during the trial, a unique system Judge Schacter allowed in his court. If at any time during the trial a juror wanted a witness to answer a question, they could write it out and submit it to the bailiff at a break. Either Ezzell or I would then ask the witness the question without revealing its source.

Many of the questions seemed to fully support that some of my points had sunk in over the months. For example, while Blake was on the stand, he testified the reason he never attempted to physically comfort Bonny was that the police kept him away. One juror pointed out Blake's anger towards me on the stand, and asked,

"Had you used that anger at the crime scene and demanded to be allowed to be near your wife, do you think you would have prevailed? Why did we not see you trying to comfort your injured wife? Surely she deserved at least a (perhaps last) 'goodbye toots.'"

Another question to Blake from the jury related to his trial testimony, in which he had said that the reason he did not use Bonny's cell phone to call for help was he did not know how to use one. I had drilled Blake on this issue, with confirmation from several sources that he *had* used cell phones prior to the murder. One juror's question read:

"Mr. Blake: You know how to shoot a gun, not an easy task. You memorized your scripts over the years and know how to make a phone call. Which part of using a cell phone did you find hard to master: 1. Flipping the phone, 2. dialing 911, or 3. hitting send?"

The wait for the verdict took so long that Ezzell had time to fly to Portugal for a two-week vacation and *still* make it back for the live verdict. (I am sure he was thrilled how that worked out!) While we waited, Ezzell's "helper" got braver with the media.

On the second week, she gave a riveting quote to Court TV: "It's like the Tom Petty song, 'The waiting is the hardest part.'" When I saw this, I could not resist mocking the shit out of her. I immediately wisecracked to Court TV, "It's like the Kansas song 'Dust in the Wind.' All we are is dust in the wind!"

The day of the verdict, I arrived to a packed courthouse laced with extra security. At around 11:30 a.m., three slow and deliberate buzzes blasted from the jury room—the jury had reached a verdict. The court announced the decision would be read after lunch, and that we were all to return at 1:30 p.m.

Two more hours and we would know. A very long two hours.

At 1:31 p.m., the jury was let into the courtroom. The judge wasted no time. "We are back on the record on the Blake matter. I understand the jury has reached its decision. Mr. Foreperson, please hand the jury's verdict to the clerk."

The clerk opened the verdict and began to read to an absolutely dead-silent courtroom,

"We, the jury, find as follows: Question 1. Did Robert Blake intentionally cause the death of Bonny Lee Bakley on May 4, 2001?

"YES."

I broke down and began to cry. My intern put his arm around me as I waited for the next few sentences from the clerk, words that would forever change my life. "What are the total damages of the Estate of Bonny Lee Bakley from May 4, 2001, through today's date and reasonably expected to be suffered in the future?

"30 MILLION DOLLARS."

I WON—I FUCKING WON *BIG TIME!*

The tears were freely flowing as I mouthed to each juror member with soul-wrenching gratitude, "Thank you, thank you so much!" My intern leaned over and said, "Dude, stop crying and get your composure, you are the biggest fucking stud trial lawyer in America!"

I looked up at him with a big, exhausted, dry smile.

I then had a chance to talk to both the jury and the media. First, I stepped outside to speak briefly with the press. I did not know it at the time, but when I later watched the footage from the press conference, I saw that my face was absolutely drained of all color—white as a sheet. Even the TV commentators observed how wiped out I appeared.

I then went back inside and was taken to a separate courtroom where the jury was assembled, waiting to talk to me—alone. I had limited time because the media was all waiting to talk with them as well.

Blake and Ezzell skipped out the back in complete silence and in utter devastation. Ezzell's failure to say a word to me after the jury rendered its verdict said everything!

One of my favorite memories from the day of the verdict was of my two best friends, Gary and Danny, who were driving on the 405 freeway to see a customer when the verdict was announced live on LA radio. They said when the clerk read that I proved Blake killed Bonny, they both screamed like madmen for me: "He did it, he did it!" A few seconds later, when they announced the jury's verdict to be 30 million dollars, they said they *almost lost control of the car!*

You've gotta love your friends!

Although my mom would be gone within a year, she lived long enough to see me bask in the glory of this big win! A realization of a dream we both had when she struggled to help put me through law school.

The *L.A. Times* would end up giving me a prestigious profile, and the picture they chose was an older picture I had never seen before. It was of me speaking at a press conference at my office building, and in the exact center of the picture, you can see my mom wearing a white hat.

It was the only day in four years my mom was able to travel from Michigan to see me in action, and magically this was the one picture out of hundreds chosen for the article.

THE AFTERMATH

After the verdict was rendered on November 18, 2005, several major events occurred. The most dramatic was Judge Schacter had some form of seizure following the trial and took a major medical leave of absence. Aside from the obvious concern for this man I had come to really like and completely respect, the verdict form was left unsigned from November until early February 2006.

Blake used this as an opportunity to try and void the 30-million-dollar verdict by filing for bankruptcy before the judge was well enough to sign the verdict. Blake brought back my old nemesis, Gerald Schwartzbach, to also file a massive motion for a new trial, separate from the bankruptcy.

The way I found out about all of this was through a call I received from the *L.A. Times* out of the blue, when I was blindsided with the question: Robert Blake just filed for bankruptcy a few hours ago and seeks to void the unsigned judgment—what is your response?

I had no idea about any of this, and winged the following quoted response for the morning paper:

"The concept of Robert Blake filing bankruptcy in an effort to avoid paying the 30-million-dollar judgment is something that was highly anticipated and we are ready."

The bankruptcy judge denied the motion to void the judgment, ruling that the verdict would have been easily signed if the trial judge had not fallen ill. After the bankruptcy judge ruled, Blake was left with the sole option of seeking a new trial motion through Schwartzbach.

By now, Mr. "I-don't-do-press-conferences" Schwartzbach was all over the news badmouthing me again. He was quoted in the *L.A. Times* saying, "From what I hear, Dubin won despite himself." He held a press conference and stated, "We are excited to file the new trial motion which I believe is extremely meritorious."

Here is a guy coming back into the case—for free—claiming that I was the one doing it doing for the media attention?

The first time I found out the grounds Schwartzbach was seeking the new trial on, was again in the media. I read the following headline on Google:

"BLAKE LAWYERS CLAIM 'JURY MISCONDUCT' ASK JUDGE TO THROW OUT 30 MILLION DOLLAR VERDICT."

The next day, I got a massive box delivered from Schwartzbach with his 2000-page motion, exhibits, and court reporter transcripts. Schwartzbach had sent out his private investigators to meet with the jurors and dig up any dirt possible to support a new trial.

A quick reading of the motion was all the media needed to go crazy with the story, treating it like bombshell new developments. On a more important note, I only had a few days to review, research, find the jurors, and file my opposition to the new trial motion.

I had no clue where these jurors were except for one juror who wrote me a letter commending my trial performance. Obviously the Blake lawyers were not going to tell me where the jurors lived and I also could not get this information from the court.

The next morning, I hit the mother lode. I managed to get in touch with the main juror who had signed Schwartzbach's prepared statement, which the defense was basing their entire motion around. Turns out she had no idea she was being used to support a new trial motion for Blake, and truly believed it was a fair trial with no jury misconduct.

In total, within 48 hours I was able to obtain statements from seven of the jurors, denying the allegations in Schwartzbach's motion. I had no idea how the judge would ultimately rule on Friday, but I felt pretty solid about the work I had done. I returned the favor to the Blake lawyers by e-mailing a copy of my opposition to the media, resulting in the headline: "BLAKE JURORS DENY MISCONDUCT."

When Schwartzbach was asked for his response to my powerful opposition that included jurors' denying any and all charges of misconduct, he stated, "I have not yet seen Mr. Dubin's papers."

I also had my first communication from Ezzell since the trial ended, a little zinger that highlighted his lingering bitterness. He had e-mailed me his FedEx number to mail him some documents he had requested, to which I responded by thanking him and joking that money was still tight. His response was textbook Ezzell. "Best not count on getting any from Blake."

You would think I would be really nervous with such a huge motion coming up that Friday, with literally everything on the line once again. Losing that motion against Schwartzbach and Ezzell would have wiped away everything I had accomplished, and it would have been a total nightmare to do another trial. It was also Judge Schacter's first week back on the bench after a five-month medical leave, and I had no idea how good his health would be. (He was thankfully fine!)

On my way up to Burbank, I decided to stop by my office to make sure the Blake lawyers did not sucker punch me with any last minute paperwork. They did! They had filed a new 20-page opposition, in addition to objections to every single juror statement I had. I grabbed the new stuff and read it over, holding my breath for any new bombshells they might drop.

My final battle would be a tag-team match against Schwartzbach and Ezzell—they would be arguing the motion together at the hearing. Schwartzbach started the argument stating that he had never seen such outrageous jury misconduct in his 30 years of practicing law. He pleaded with Judge Schacter to throw out what he kept calling a "tainted" verdict.

After 35 minutes of arguing his case, Schwartzbach passed the baton to Ezzell who continued for another 30 minutes, again giving his absolute best.

I spent 30 minutes responding to all the points they had both raised, and answering any questions Judge Schacter had brought up.

Judge Schacter gave no feedback, and did not make a decision on the motion. Instead, he took the matter under submission over the weekend and issued his ruling on Monday. That weekend's wait was worse than the jury deliberations.

On Monday, I received a phone call from the court clerk, the same person who had read the jury verdict out loud, and in a very strained voice he began telling me that the judge had issued his ruling. He explained he thought it was best to call me directly so I would hear about it before the media.

I WAS DYING!

He kept going with this preamble for what was probably two minutes, but felt like five weeks. Finally, at the very end, in a monotone voice he said, "The court has denied the motion."

Victory, at last!

CHAPTER 22

FULL CIRCLE—
THE TELEVISED BRONCO CHASE

In part, "Reality TV" was born on the back seat of a white Ford Bronco on a Los Angeles freeway, capturing a gun-toting O.J. Simpson hiding on the car floor, while being simultaneously followed by the LAPD and millions of Americans glued to their TV screens. Even more importantly, the televised low-speed chase was one of the first indicators of the extent of the media's influence over the potential jury pool watching.

Before the Bronco chase, many people across America truly believed our beloved sports hero, O.J. Simpson, was flat-out innocent. We all felt like we knew him, and he just seemed too nice and gentle a man to be capable of such a horrific crime. He was O.J. the football legend, O.J. the Hertz spokesman, *O.J. from the Naked Gun movies!*

Then, on a Friday afternoon in June 1994 everything changed! First, the LAPD went on TV and reported O.J. had disappeared, failing to turn himself in before an agreed upon 11 a.m. deadline. You could feel the complete shock and disbelief electrifying America; even the media at the press conference appeared to be rattled.

O.J. is a fugitive?

Then his lawyer made a public plea for O.J to turn himself in, and there was even talk of a suicide note left behind. It was heartbreaking, like a punch in the gut to everyone who loved O.J. Simpson, a wakeup call none of his millions of fans wanted. It was like all of America collectively realized: *"Wow, he really did it!"*

I was working for a law firm at the time, and we all huddled into the conference room to watch the live coverage of O.J.'s disappearance. Many of the attorneys I worked with went to USC—where O.J. played his college ball and won the Heisman Award—were almost crying watching the coverage. They were devastated at the realization their hero was a murderer, and was either going to go to prison or end his life.

In my opinion, the Bronco chase was the *defining moment* in believing O.J. was guilty of the crime. Anybody who was speaking out about O.J. "never being able to do something like this" went silent after that slow-speed chase and police standoff. Even O.J.'s buddy and ABC sportscaster, Al Michaels, stayed quiet after the dramatic arrest!

I remember leaving work to go home and watch the coverage. It was such a huge event that NBC used split-screen coverage to follow the Bronco chase along with the primetime NBA Finals. All I could think of during the low-speed Bronco chase was, *O.J., why did you do this?* I mean, any thought or hope of his innocence went right out the window.

The Bronco chase was such a mammoth part of American pop culture that *USA Today* recently named it one of the top five most memorable bookmarks of our time.

In retrospect, one of the most fascinating things about the Bronco chase was how the prosecutors presented this *historic* event to the jury.

They never mentioned it!

One of the top five moments in our lives, *yet the jury that acquitted O.J. never heard a word mentioned about that police chase and climactic arrest.* The televised turning point for millions of Americans was never even mentioned to the only 12 that mattered.

Was it admissible? Absolutely! In fact, a California Jury Instruction states that jurors can view flight by defendants as evidence of guilt.

Apparently the D.A. did not fully comprehend the power of the media, and how the white Bronco chase was the public's prevailing visual of the entire trial. The jury obviously knew about it, just as the rest of the planet did, and must have wondered why the prosecutors never even mentioned it. The D.A. turned a blind eye to an epic media event that had tainted the jury pool, even though the taint most likely favored their chance of conviction.

I had a chance to speak with then Los Angeles D.A. Gil Garcetti a short time after the O.J. trial, and asked him specifically why he chose not to introduce the Bronco chase for the jury to consider.

He told me that during the entire police chase O.J. was on the phone with his mother, and was making self-serving statements about his innocence that may have helped the defense. He felt that telling the jury about the chase, (and passport, money and gun found in the Bronco) "would open the door to all the statements between O.J. and his mom on the phone."

So they chose not to use it, and left it on the bench.

In the name of Monday morning quarterbacks around the world, maybe not the best call, Gil.

Now, the media has become so interjected into these high profile cases, their helicopters not only cover defendants fleeing from the law, *they also cover them driving to court for trial!* It was like the start of the Kentucky Derby once Judge Ito opened up his courtroom for the world to join in. We now have twenty-four-hour news coverage, real time courtroom bloggers, and same-day trial re-enactments on entertainment channels.

And it all started with the Bronco chase!

ABOUT THE AUTHOR

"To Eric, who can beat me!"
—Famed Trial Attorney Gerry Spence

I always dreamed of winning a huge case of the Blake magnitude, and of course, doing so in glorious style. I was not going to let a small detail, like being absurdly out-gunned by Blake's legal team, interfere with what I had always done—WIN!

Not many lawyers do litigation, yet alone jury trials. But for me, it was all I wanted to do. As a boy, I wanted to be the one up at the plate in the bottom of the ninth, with the bases loaded. I always felt like I could come through with that game-winning hit for my team. I still feel that way!

I was born and raised in Oak Park, Michigan, a suburb outside of Detroit, and was the clear underachiever in my family. My older brother of two years was a mathematical genius, who carved out an early academic path I clearly chose to ignore. I remember my teachers would not even try to mask their disappointment in me, saying things like, "You're Bruce Dubin's brother?" as if I was posing.

I had an amazing and loving mom, and my grandparents lived right down the street behind my elementary school.

Everyday at lunch I would cut through the baseball field to their house, and watch *Happy Days* while my grandma made me grilled cheese sandwiches. Both our kids are named after my grandfather, gone for 30 years, but still on my mind almost every day.

My father often tells the story about my kindergarten parent/teacher conference, when he met with the same teacher who had taught my brother a few years earlier. My father was seated along with my mother in the miniature kindergarten-sized seats, and claims he almost fell backwards when the teacher proclaimed, "In my 20 years of teaching kindergarten, your son is the absolute worst child I have ever had."

I was next kicked out of first grade for playing hooky, spending the entire second grade with the special education students after being labeled a "behavioral problem." I was placed back in the regular classes from third grade on, after being considered "rehabilitated."

I also always dreamed of living in California, and transferred west to the University of Arizona for a business degree. I met my wife Dalia in college, and we have been together ever since. I next went to California Western School of Law in San Diego. I became crazy serious during my first year, studying 16 hours a day and finishing the first year of law school ranked 13 out of about 350 students in my class.

Even with amazing grades, the competition for the big jobs in California was outrageous with every superstar law student from Harvard to Stanford applying. I sent hundreds or résumés to every single big law firm only to get dozens of reject letters daily. Quite often I would get combination reject letters from the really big firms that read: "Thank you for your letters and résumés sent to our Los Angeles, San Francisco and San Diego offices. The answer is no to all. *Please stop writing now, we will keep your résumé on file.*"

So, like most who came out of law school in California's poor legal job market in 1992, I took the first job I could get. I grabbed a low-paying job working for a large civil defense firm in downtown Los Angeles. When I asked the 75-year-old senior partner for more money during the hiring interview, he pulled out a huge stack of first year résumés and said, "You want it or not?"

Fuck yes! I'll take it!

I was trained by a burned-out trial lawyer, who had made a living out of winning cases during the 70s and 80s, high on coke and drunk on vodka. We would have lunch and he would detail outrageous stories of him doing coke in the courthouse bathroom during trial breaks. In fact, he said he later had major concerns about going to trial sober because he was so successful whacked out on blow and Smirnoff.

My boss gave me virtually all his cases right off the bat. I took around a hundred depositions in my first year, and was in charge of 30 cases without the faintest idea what I was doing. Literally I had no clue, and relied on my experienced legal secretary and my new buddy, Charles, a third-year lawyer with the firm.

Being thrown in head-first forced me to excel to stay afloat, and I became really good, really fast. I also became very used to being the youngest and least experienced lawyer in the room, and learned never to let that appear to be a factor.

There are no handicaps in lawyering, the best lawyer wins—straight up.

The firm eventually went down (no surprise considering there were highly questionable billing practices) and I jumped ship to a smaller defense firm, Murtaugh, Miller, Meyer and Nelson in Orange County, California. There I became the firm's go-to pit bull lawyer, known for winning the hard cases. I had a remarkable mentor in Rick Meyer, and Mike Murtaugh is still a friend I count on for advice.

I remember winning my first jury trial for a security guard company sued for beating up an armed suspect after a late night shooting at a gang-filled apartment complex. Even though four police officers testified that my clients used excessive force in restraining the gun-toting plaintiff, I won the trial using the old "he fell into a tree" defense. My theme to the jury was "bullets kill," and these hired security guards in dangerous gang areas do not go home alive to their families after work if they gently ask suspects, "Can I please have the gun, pretty please?"

At 32 years old, I had a gut feeling that I could make it on my own and decided to give it a shot. With one case and only $5000 to my name, I gave notice to open up my own law firm, "The Law Office of Eric J. Dubin."

I still remember the concerned look on my boss's face after I resigned, but asked him if I could stay on an extra week for the money. "Eric, if one week's salary is going to help make a difference in your new practice," he said, "you really need to re-think your decision."

He was not wrong, but my law firm thrived!

My marketing strategy for my new firm was simple: complete blind faith! Right away, the cases started rolling in, coming from attorneys I had worked with or gone up against in the past. I kept getting and winning really difficult cases others thought could not be won.

One of the first solo cases I won was for an 11-year-old girl who had been attacked in a fast food restaurant restroom. She came from a very hard background, yet had this amazing smile and inspiring courage beyond her years. Even though I was flat broke,

I took my recovered fee from her case and bought her a full computer setup for her schoolwork. After it arrived, she called me uncontrollably crying, saying "you don't understand, nobody has ever done something like this from me before—ever!" (Who said lawyers are all bad?) Years later, she invited me to sit with her family for her high school graduation. Priceless!

In 1997, I was invited to meet and train with the legendary trial lawyer Gerry Spence at a secluded mountain retreat in Palomar, California, an invitation that to me was the equivalent of being asked to train with the Jedi master of jury trials.

I had first met Spence a few years back at a California State Bar conference in Napa Valley when I was still a defense lawyer, where he told me about his trial school and that he only trained plaintiff lawyers. Over the next three years, every November I would go to master my craft with Spence and some of the best lawyers in the world, including Milton Grimes.

I remember one night during the first year, I was sitting next to (my hero) Spence at dinner. I leaned over and jokingly whispered, "I could beat you!" Spence just gave me back a warm smile as if to say, "that's cute, I am sure you could."

I would learn from Gerry the invaluable lesson that exposing your flaws to a jury with complete openness and honesty is where the *real* power lies. People don't go to the theater to see if the "perfect actor" memorized their lines, they want to be moved by the magic of the story. In fact, when an actor makes a big mistake on stage, for example dropping a prop, letting the audience in on the moment is pure gold.

Over the years, I had really hoped Spence had forgotten about my comment to him at dinner, a hope Gerry finally squashed when he presented me with a copy of his new book in which he wrote to me:

"To Eric—who can beat me."

Years later, after Robert Blake was arrested and placed in jail awaiting trial, a rumor broke out that Gerry Spence would be taking over for Blake. I held my breath when I heard Spence had met with Robert Blake at the L.A. County Jail to discuss handling the murder trial for him.

Spence subsequently passed. I exhaled.

DEDICATION

This book is dedicated to my amazing family!

To my truly magical daughter, Alexa (who types as follows: *my dad rocks, love Alexa to Daddy*), and precious son Jakob ("my little man"). Being a dad to you both is surely what heaven must feel like! I love you both, and could not be more proud to be your dad!

My beautiful wife Dalia, the love of my life. You are my heart. I am so lucky; you were always too good for me, and still are!

My best friend, Gary Lerner. ("A friend walks in when the rest of the world walks out."—Anonymous). You are simply one of life's blessings! Thank you, brother!

My confidante and uncle, David Benigsohn, who has never let me down! You were *always* my "favorite" uncle!

Danny Straus, football pool aside, thank you for always caring so much—you're a great friend. Kappy, thank you buddy!

Carrie and Roy Krauthamer, thanks for being great cousins and friends. David Balamut and Harv Freed, my Michigan boys! D.J. Millet, Rick and Susan Meyer, Mike Murtaugh, Roger Grant, Joe Kaneda, Dayna Lerner, Ron and Laurie Resch, Alison and David Ursu, Debbie Cohn, Elaine Schreiber, Joni Pick, Stacey Pacelli, Sue Westover and Dale Giali, Wes and Jody Pierce, Jeremy Popoff, Sheri Suglia, Glenn Gelman, Brian B., Rick Steinberg, my Sunday morning SHM boys, Alan Gorde, and Richard and Sharon Bockoff. Thank you, Chloe!

Holly, Glenn, it was an honor to sit next to you everyday. You both showed class and courage beyond your years, I am sure Bonny would have been very proud—I was! Margerry, thank you for everything, together we got justice and set the record straight! Blanchard, you are a good man!

Also to the Los Angeles D.A.'s office and prosecutors, Shellie Samuels and Greg Dohi. L.A. Robbery Homicide Detectives Ron Ito, Brian Tyndall, and Steve Eguchi. Thank you for the privilege of presenting all your hard work, I hope I did you all proud. I have never met finer people!

Jean and Andrew, thank you. Tim Conway Jr., *you da man!*

A huge thank you to Henrietta for being so great, patient, and fun to work with! You rock! Thank you, Ariana! Thank you, Sonia, for your amazing cover art. And to Michael Viner and Phoenix Books, I am very proud to have worked with you on both this book and Larry King's *Beyond a Reasonable Doubt.* Thank you so much for all your support.

Love to my father, Marvin Dubin, my brother Bruce, and their families.

To Bert Stahl, thank you for making my mom so happy; she died surrounded by love.

Jules and Jennie Benigsohn. My aunt Ronna Benigsohn.

Finally, this book is in loving memory of my mom, Lynn Dubin Stahl. Mom, I love you, thank you for always believing in me—even without good reason. I miss you!

I now and forever understand what unconditional love is!